Johanna

SURVIVOR
OF
THE HOLOCAUST
AND
SIBERIA

As Told to Joan Davies
Edited by Bishop Thomas J. Connolly

Copyright © 2003
Bishop Thomas J. Connolly

All rights reserved. No part of the material protected by this copyright notice may be reproduced or utilized in any form or by any means, electronic or mechanical, including photocopying, recording, or by any informational storage and retrieval system, without written permission from the copyright owner.

ISBN: 0-9740557-0-0

Published by:
TWILIGHT BOOKS
PO Box 5999
Bend, OR 97708

Printed in the United States of America by
Maverick Publications, Inc. • Bend, Oregon

Contents

Dedication	v
Preface	vi
Foreword	viii
1. My First Year in Prison	1
2. Saved by Recollections of my Childhood	15
3. Condemned to Rothenfeld Prison	27
4. Rothenfeld Prisoner #696	40
5. From Prison to Concentration Camp for Life	51
6. Ravensbrück – Concentration Camp for #20442	59
7. The Camp at its Worst	73
8. The Warsaw Loot Place	83
9. To Siberia & Prison Number 47	96
10. Escape from Siberia	110
11. My Son, My Son…	123
Epilogue	129
Postscript	133

Johanna Köster, 1977.

DEDICATION

In admiration and respect, this book is dedicated to the memory of Johanna and all those who suffered from the oppression of the Nazi and Communist regimes.

Lest we forget!

☦ *Thomas J. Connolly*

July 30, 2004

To my Sister Phyllis,

Happy Birthday; and wishing you many, many more. Hope that you find it spiritually uplifting.

With Love in Christ,
Bryan and Laila
Megan and Vina

Preface

I have, on a number of occasions, heard Johanna Köster tell the gripping story of her nine years of confinement; one year in a German prison, four years in a concentration camp in Germany, from which she was released when the Russians invaded Germany, only to be sent to Siberia for four more years. She always began her story by saying, "What I have to tell you will not be easy for you to listen to, nor easy for me to tell you, but I hope that it will be helpful for you in your journey of faith. In the darkest days of my suffering, in the midst of personal hunger, sickness, loneliness, exposure, beatings, when all strength was gone and I preferred to die, God became real. I felt His presence, and He comforted me."

It is my hope that all who read this book may similarly experience the power of God to transform the useless frustration of suffering into redemptive life both here and hereafter.

I first met Johanna in California where she was living at that time. She was working in the accounting department of a cardboard box factory. She proudly told me that her department was the top of the class. It was typical of Johanna. Everything she did had to be first class.

I had heard her story from a priest-friend who was working with me at a leadership camp for high school students in the San Bernardino Mountains. The story thrilled me and I asked if I could meet this extraordinary person. The priest kindly arranged a meeting; I became close friends with Johanna and since she was looking for a new place to live because she was suffering from the smog, I invited her to come to Baker, Oregon. She came to visit in 1977 and fell in love with the clean air, the open spaces and the Elkhorn Mountains.

I had the privilege of finding a house for her to live in, and ultimately seeing her into eternal life.

The book you are reading was first told to Joan Davies, then with some re-editing by me, is finally printed. I am grateful to Mary Ann Davis and her brother Thomas for scanning, typing and arranging the text to make it more readable. I hope that you enjoy reading it as much as I have in bringing it to you. I am convinced that it is a story that must be told.

☦ *Thomas J. Connolly*
Bishop Emeritus of the Diocese of Baker

Foreword

Why am I writing this book? After all, it is more than 30 years since I returned to civilization and was able to build a new life. Why do I dig up horrible memories of the years that deprived me of my rights as a human being, and inflicted every possible humiliation on me? Should I, as a Christian, just "forgive and forget"?

It is not my intention to revive or keep alive any hatred of those who tortured me. We cannot make the world better by hatred. Time has a wonderful ability to smooth out "wrinkles" in our feelings and emotions. As callous as it may sound, it is true that time heals all wounds, and I could not live with myself if I were filled with hatred.

I am writing this book to show my fellowmen who have been hit by hardships where to look for the strength to endure them. I was fortunate enough to find Christ in the prisons and concentration camps of Germany and Russia, and I am convinced that the good Lord let me survive so that I could bring this message to others. I have given talks to church groups of many denominations and I know that I have touched several people.

If I can help any of my readers in the same way, then this book has served its purpose. —*Johanna*

CHAPTER ONE

My First Year in Prison

"...hallowed be Thy name. Thy kingdom come, Thy will be done, on earth as it is in heaven..." The words were spoken in Polish and at the top of her tremulous voice. I could see her approaching the wooden steps that led to the entrance two floors below me. Her arms bound, the woman held her head high, repeating the words firmly and loudly to give her strength. The tall guard beside her spoke curtly in German, motioning to hurry. Her steps lengthened, her thin legs stretching against the dirty, wrinkled fabric of her dress, but she kept her back straight and began the prayer again. They passed out of sight below me and a door closed to the steady meter of her supplication.

I turned reluctantly from the barred, open window. The body heat and the smell of a dozen unwashed women hit me. I fought the nausea crowding into my dry throat, and pressed my nose and mouth against the cold smooth wall. The "one man" cell held eleven Ukrainian women and myself, with an uncovered bucket in one corner serving as our communal toilet. When I arrived, the contents had already flowed over the sides and onto the floor. I had assumed ownership of the single wooden shelf that ran along one wall. The others slept on mattresses that were delivered to us at night and taken away again in the morning.

None of my cellmates spoke Dutch or German, and I knew not one word of their language. Only occasionally could we communicate through much hand waving and charade-like gesturing. While I found myself growing more frightened and bewildered at my sudden imprisonment, these women were either confident they would soon be released, or incredibly ignorant of the significance of a Gestapo arrest. As I sat alone, startled by every strange noise in the corridor and outside, the Ukrainians played a game of "tag". They stood in a circle, backs to each other, waiting for one woman to tag another on the back. If the tagged player couldn't guess who had touched her, she became "it".

I sat on the rough-cut plank, my limited island of security, pulled my legs under me and closed my eyes wearily. Oh God, dear God. Why? What is happening to my world? What will they do to me? What have they done with my Frans, and my little one, our baby Frans, who looks so much like his brown-eyed papa? Oh, dear Lord, bless my precious child and keep him from harm. Keep him full of warm milk and never let him suffer from the cold. And, please, let them be lying. Don't let my husband be dead.

My thoughts came and went so fast, I put my hands to the sides of my head, as if to slow it all down, keep the day in perspective, anchor my sanity. My back ached and the pain in my legs and pelvic area was a constant dull throb, like a giant, consuming heartbeat. Sweat and grime caked my hands and face. Dried blood chafed the insides of my thighs whenever I shifted my weight on the narrow shelf.

Only days before, I had given birth to my first child, a son, Frans, named for his laughing, beloved father. Someone at the hospital called my mother and told her to come get the baby. Baby Frans, I held you for such a short time, I could see you and touch you for only moments out of the days, but you are all my world. I have dreamed of you and planned for you all these months. Your father and I imagining together how you would look, how fast you would grow, how proud you would make us. Each breath I take brings me that much closer to the day they will let me go and I can kiss your smooth, perfect skin. God let me live to see my son. With the thought, my milk-filled breasts swelled against their binding—a silent cry for the child who could not be nursed.

In a half-dazed condition, my mind floated back to the recent past, into the distant past, to make sense of where I was and what had happened...

My First Year in Prison

Frans and I had been underground for almost a year before they caught us. Germany had attacked Holland May 10, 1940. I awoke to the sound of planes—many planes—and lay for a moment, wondering if I were still asleep and dreaming the roar. Germany and England were at war, but the Dutch hadn't flown all winter. I ran to the window of my third floor bedroom and leaned out into the pre-dawn darkness, staring incredulously as one gray form after another flew over the city. A floor below me, Mama opened the door to the stairs.

"Mother! What is this?"

Her face was somber and she turned grieving eyes up to me.

"Child, this means war."

"But who? Who is making war on us?"

She was strongly anti-Nazi, yet she was German herself, and she was so ashamed. "It is my-people who behave so badly here." From the beginning, we knew it was hopeless—tiny Holland against land-hungry Hitler's German forces. Frans was an officer in the Dutch air force, stationed not far from my home. We used to joke about the inadequacy of Holland's airborne defenders. I remember one day Frans told me that he had lined up his troops for inspection that morning, and I said, "Oh? One guy or both of them?" In love, we could not hear the war drums of the Third Reich, nor know the effect the Nazis would have on all our lives.

Frans came to the house on that day of invasion. "We are going to fight, but there is no chance for us to win," he explained. "The moment the war is over, you and I have to go underground. Even if the forces give up, we'll fight in what manner we can to defend what we have—until the end. You don't say to a person who comes into your house and intends to be the boss—'Alright, you are welcome to everything I have'—no, we'll fight until the last moment."

I had written articles telling the truth about Nazism before the Germans ever came to Holland, and we knew that I would be interrogated and very likely imprisoned because of those papers. Frans, an officer who also worked in the state department, could not flee with the rest of the government, so he, too, was in danger.

The war for Holland lasted five days. On Tuesday, it was over. The Germans bombed Rotterdam—a great harbor, but of no military importance—and the whole center of the city was wiped out in forty or forty-five minutes; Holland capitulated. It came over the radio, and we knew that it meant the Nazis were in complete control of the Dutch.

During that short week of war, I withdrew money and jewelry from the bank, burning any papers or books at home that I thought might cause trouble for my mother. I made a few cautious calls to friends and relatives, telling them of our plans and our need of contacts, food sources and meeting places. Then, within a week of the country's surrender, Frans and I "vanished", beginning our life together in the twilight world of the underground, going from one place to another in the semi-darkness of dusk or dawn, or the unlit blackness of night. Always thinking before making a move, never knowing for sure that we could trust the person who held our lives in his hands.

About a month and a half after Frans and I had gone underground, I was visiting friends when a man named Ben Scheppers approached me. He mentioned the name of a mutual friend from Ascona whom I knew to be quite patriotic and strongly anti-Nazi. Guido and I, as well as the rest of our post-college group, had often discussed the Nazi party, because in the spring of 1939 the rumblings of European war were like a volcano reactivating itself, ready to spew fiery death. My friend had given Ben my name and address in Holland, assuring him that I would be willing to do resistance work, but I felt I had to discuss such a serious move with Frans first, and Ben agreed. Frans was enthusiastic at once, of course. He had been trying to find a trustworthy connection in the underground since May, but the Dutch resistance wasn't organized, and he was impatient with waiting.

Ben told us he was working directly with London. He had a helper named Johan van Monken who would also be working with us, he added. We agreed to cooperate, and I was provided with a false passport and matching identification papers in the name of Laura Carp. It was my job to travel to Germany with little dictionaries—the first half was French-German, the second half German-French translations—and contact French prisoners of war who had expressed a desire to escape from Germany. Ben supplied the addresses, and I never knew where the information originated.

Some of the Kriegsgefangenen did street work, and I would walk past them, whistling "La Marseillaise", a pre-arranged signal that I was there and they should get hold of me. Or, perhaps I would stop to look in a shop window, somebody chancing to come up next to me; or I might slip down a side street for the rendezvous, if the area was nearly deserted.

The French prisoners of war weren't heavily guarded during the day, because the Germans didn't have the personnel to keep

My First Year in Prison

a close watch, although at night they were locked up in barracks surrounded by barbed wire. They could work in factories, on the streets or for nearby farmers. Farm workers could stay nights on the farm, as long as the windows of their rooms were secured with wire because if these Frenchmen were to escape, they could never make it through the German countryside with no knowledge of the language, and a big "KG" painted on the back of their clothing, identifying them as Kriegsgefangenen—war prisoners. That was where I came in.

I taught them the rudiments of German, the proper accent and pronunciation, and obtained civilian clothes for them. Somebody else got them over the border, for I only prepared them for escape. Frans and I together undertook a heartbreaking, yet life-giving task. Jewish babies and children were given into our keeping by grieving parents who believed arrest and transportation to a concentration camp were imminent. The excruciating pain of separating their children from themselves was overridden by the knowledge of what was almost assuredly in store for them. Each of the tiny, persecuted Jews was placed with a farm family in Holland—good people willing to take the children in and raise them as their own. It was their only chance of survival.

The first months of German occupation hardly altered the Dutch way of life, compared to the hardships that came later in the war. Prominent young men and civic leaders were imprisoned, of course, and the Nazi policy was that if any German soldier came to harm, or if there was any real breach of Nazi rule, a half-dozen young Dutchmen met their deaths on the same day. One of the first things the Nazis did was to confiscate all motor vehicles and then all radios. Two stations, controlled by the Nazis, were piped in. Having an independent, or concealed, radio was punishable by banishment to a Konzentrationslager—concentration camp.

Reich marshal, Herman Goring, conducted the establishment of the concentration camps, which were first created for the confinement of thousands of Communists and Social Democratic Party leaders. Members of the Catholic faith, and the Church itself, soon became Party enemies, as did the Jews. The camps' purpose enlarged to include individuals who opposed the Nazi Party, whether through their beliefs or their actions. In the 1938 anti-Jewish pogrom, more than 20,000 Jews were taken into "protective custody" by the Gestapo, and sent to concentration camps. Six major camps came into being during the next year:

Buchenwald, Dachau, Flossenburg, Mauthausen, Sachsenhausen and Ravensbrück.

The largest part of Germany's working force was in uniform, so the Nazis resorted to prison labor to keep the nation's factories operating. Nine more camps were established between 1940 and 1942, and thousands of laborers were transported in from German-occupied countries to be housed in the concentration camps—"KZs"—and auxiliary labor camps. Prominent citizens all over Europe disappeared under the Nacht und Nebel Erlass—night and fog decree—and were secretly imprisoned in the camps. The KZs were under the administration of an office of the Schutzstaffel —SS—and were guarded, for the most part, by special SS units called Totenkopfverbande—death's head battalions.

The Dutch Jews were faced with immediate and terrifying changes as the occupation forces moved in. Down the street from my mother's house lived a Jewish family named Frankenberg. They owned an office supply and stationery store, and I remember Mr. Frankenberg offering me a pencil or eraser as a gift when I came to his store as a child. Luckily for him, he died before he had to see his family deported to Auschwitz. His wife jumped from the train on the way to the camp and was killed. Another Dutch Jew spent the entirety of World War II in a hole in the ground in one of Holland's forests. As a result, he became tragically crippled with arthritis, but he was, at least, alive.

Frans and I wanted to be married, as we had planned, but in Holland, law requires that couples marry first in the town hall under the auspices of the burgomaster or some other town official. If the couple wants to marry in a church, also, they can, but the religious ceremony is not legally binding. We couldn't go to the town hall without giving ourselves away, so we spoke to the pastor of my church, who was also a good friend of the family. He promised to marry us in the sacristy of his church, risking his life to do so, and our secret wedding took place on July 20, 1940.

We didn't live together in a house like other married couples, because, officially, we didn't exist. Neither could we go to the office where ration cards were issued. We depended completely on the discretion of those hiding us, and we were constantly a burden, an addition to their peril. And, there was always the fear that perhaps we didn't know our friends quite as well as we had thought. Or it could be a neighbor or the milkman who noticed a face at the window or who wondered about an order for an extra bottle of milk.

My husband was a wonderful man. He was compassionate, gentle and understanding, with a strong character and ever-present sense of humor. He always brought me a gift when we were reunited following our frequent separations because of resistance work, or when we split up to be less of a burden on the people hiding us. It could be a piece of candy, or a bright flower he picked along the road. I loved his brown eyes because they were so different from the blue eyes of my family, and he was so good-looking I often wondered how I could have caught such a perfect man. He was everything I wanted in a husband—there was nothing I wanted to change about him.

Both of us were sexually inexperienced. I was brought up very strictly, and there was never any talk of sex. I had three married sisters, but they would never have talked about their sex lives—it was taboo. But Frans was tender and understanding. I couldn't have asked for anyone more loving. Both of us were Catholic and we believed human life was sacred, that children were a gift from God. We didn't use contraceptives—we didn't really know what they were.

In August, I discovered I was pregnant and our lives took on another serious dimension. Fortunately for us, I suffered no real discomfort from my condition, other than allowing for my extra bulk as the days flew by. We spent as much time together as we possibly could, sometimes pretending we were just an average Dutch couple who would wake in the morning to a peaceful, back to normal Holland.

We were to spend Christmas 1940 in Amsterdam with friends, but at the last moment, we were afraid to endanger them. The Nazis had enforced a 9 p.m. curfew when they first came, and now they were making raids in the middle of the night. Soldiers would surround a block and houses were searched. Anyone who tried to escape was shot.

We went out during the day, traveling towards my home town, scurrying from the road at the slightest sound, waiting in the undergrowth like animals while cars or wagons or single horses passed by. When darkness came, we were only as far as a villa community, which neighbors the town where I grew up. I could go no further. My feet ached and my toes were cold, my belly weighed three times more than it had that morning; my temples pounded, my stomach growled and my knees threatened to buckle under me.

Frans and I celebrated our first—and our only—Christmas together in an opening in some woods that bordered the village. If I stood up, I could see the lights of the houses on the edge of town, twinkling in shades of gold and white. In my mind's eye, I saw coated figures dashing up to front doors which opened on an immensity of warmth and light, laughing children, steaming bowls of holiday repast. Rejoicing.

Frans hummed as he arranged our bedding in front of the fire that struggled to survive by feeding on damp wood, as if he were at home at The Hague in front of a holly-trimmed fireplace that held a roaring fire. His agile feet seemed oblivious to the stiffening mud that sucked at our shoes. I sat miserable and lonely on a tree stump away from his activity, wishing I could be anywhere but where I was, and chiding myself for being selfish. We supped on dried fruit, chocolate and strong, hot coffee as the moon rose to focus a white, serene light on our little clearing. We had talked all day about our childhood Christmases and what my sisters and brothers would be doing for their children and Mama. The homesickness and depression got the best of me and I began to cry, first in bitter self-pity, and then in thankful love for my strong, patient Frans. But he took me in his arms and held me tight, talking and laughing to reassure me, and I soon forgot the frost and the isolation, the discomfort and weariness. I pressed my face into the roughness of his worn shirt, breathing in the comforting man smell that belonged only to Frans, feeling secure and unassailable within the circle of his arms. I thought only of the precious time I had with him, and the feel of his child moving inside me.

We sang "Silent Night" in German, its original language, and he teased me, calling me a Nazi lady because of my proper German and impassioned voice. He had a special way with words that could always bring me laughter.

The months passed and our gypsy rag-tag life began to seem like a natural way of existence. The blade of fear constantly pressing against our throats began to dull with familiarity. And then something went wrong.

I don't know if someone informed on us—you never knew, even in families, if someone could be a Nazi sympathizer—or if Frans was accidentally discovered as he made his way to me. Waiting in a friend's house, I answered the door, confident it was Frans. Instead, I faced the Gestapo.

Panic gripped me, yet I tried to remain calm outwardly, even as I fought for my breath. One of the two men on the doorstep shoved me back into the room, laughing and sneering at my fright and my cow-like awkwardness as I moved to protect my swollen belly.

"You were expecting someone else? Perhaps your husband, was it, Schmuckstuck? So maybe you wonder where he is, your wonderful man, ja? Let me tell you, he is dead. Yes, quite dead, and he danced to his execution. He must have been very happy."

The man's voice was fading, and I blinked my eyes, trying to focus on his face as he shoved his way towards me, opening his mouth wide, as if he were shouting.

"Do you hear me? You don't believe me? I assure you, he did. You see, we beat the soles of his feet so badly that he couldn't walk—so naturally he danced!"

His face, the light in the ceiling and the walls whirled in to suffocate me. I fainted and fell to the floor.

I have no recollection of the birth of my son. There is only a faint blur of pain and blood, the businesslike tone of voice the doctor and nurses used, and being moved rapidly from one room to another. The high vaulted ceilings, all in need of a paint job, were the only constant as my battered mind sought to mend itself, letting only a little of the horror in at a time. Yet I can still feel the weight of my son's tiny body in my arms, and hear his hungry cries.

Much of the time, I was out of my head, not merely from the stress of premature labor, but from shock at the thought of my husband dying in agony, and at the prospect of what could be done to me and my fatherless child. When I was awake, I thought of torture and starvation; in my dreams the same thoughts became nightmarish and greatly out of proportion.

That's when I first began reliving the wonderland of my childhood, and I sought strength from the memories of good people and unending love, and the comfort of faith and belief in God.

I remember...

The little town of Mettingen in Germany was without challenge for its young men, and in 1851 my father's father left for Holland along with several other young men. After a few years, he decided to marry and chose a girl from his native town, writing a letter to his brothers and sisters (his parents were dead by that time) to ask for their approval and blessing. After the marriage, my grandmother remained in Germany to take care of the property there, while my grandfather returned to his business in

Holland. He and his two bachelor brothers took turns in conducting their businesses in the two countries. While two of them remained in Holland, the third would spend six weeks in Germany.

My grandparents had seven children, but only two of them, my father and his older brother, were fit to live. Four died in infancy and one, August, lived until he was 37. He started life normally, but when he was seven years old, his mental and physical growth stopped. He lived with his mother until she died, after which he entered an institution until his own death a few years later.

My father joined the Holland business after he finished grammar school. His older brother was, by that time, already well established and married. About four times a year, Father returned to Germany to stay with his mother for six weeks, as his father and uncles had done for years.

He inherited a great love for the Catholic faith from his parents. They were devout, with a front door emblem carved in stone: cross, anchor and heart—faith, hope and charity. Grandfather had given his new wife a prayer book containing prayers he had composed and written out. One was "For husband in foreign country" and another was "For deceased husband". He intended to have her praying for him not only during his life, but afterwards as well.

When Father first came to Holland, there was only a little wooden church in the small town where they lived, and it had no organ. Grandfather gave an organ to the church in honor of Father's sixteenth birthday, and Father played it each Sunday while his brother directed the choir (a handful of their employees).

Father attended Mass every morning at seven, no matter how busy he was. Even on a business trip to choose new collections for his clothing business, he would ask the hotel clerk to wake him in time to visit the nearest Catholic Church. He received Communion only on Sunday morning. The night before, he didn't sleep, but prayed all night, in order to prepare himself. After he married, he attended early Mass, High Mass and Benediction.

But he was not a holier-than-thou man. He was outgoing, warm, musical and fond of theater and beer. When he was in Germany, and friends visited, they sometimes wanted to drink a glass of wine, but my grandmother was very strict and did not approve of this, so they would send "little brother," August, to the cellar to get the wine. They soon discovered that August always first took his pipe to the cellar, and they asked him why. With all the reasoning and clear logic of a seven-year-old, August confided that he had established this method of deception so that "if Mother asks me what I'm doing in the cellar, I can say I'm looking for my pipe."

When Father was in his thirties, he decided that he should also marry and start a business of his own. His brother already had five children, two of them sons, who would soon join the firm. Several years before, Father had met a Prussian nobleman, Count Anton Wardeck von Sodembourg, who had invited him to his estate for a wild boar hunt. They liked each other and whenever Father went to Berlin on business, he would travel to East Prussia to spend a few days with his friend and the Wardeck family.

The castle had been given to the family in 1572 by Pope Pius V in recognition of their firm stand during the aftermath of the Reformation. At the same time, they were ennobled and given the title Count von Sodembourg, which was added to the family name of Wardeck. The property was quite remote—a trip to the nearest village took 45 minutes by horse and buggy.

The old gentleman had been a real monarchist and the Emperor Wilhelm II was his idol. In 1918 when Germany lost World War I, the Emperor went into exile in Holland, and the old count's world collapsed. He had been a cavalry officer most of his life, but could not serve in the War because of his rheumatism so he tried to fight the enemy from behind his beer stein. His two sons both entered the service, but the youngest died of pneumonia while still in officer's training. The older one fought in Russia, and towards the end of the war when he was home on furlough, he tried to tell his father what it was really like on the Front. "It will be impossible for us to win the war, Father, believe me."

The old soldier became so enraged that, when his son left to go back to his regiment, he did not shake hands with him. He also forbade the servants to pack his son's rucksack with ham, sausages, cheeses and bread, as was customary. The young man survived the war and came back, but the relationship was never the same, and he spent most of his life in Juterbog near Berlin.

There were six Wardeck children, and they all called Father, "uncle." It would have been considered impolite to call him by his first name, and since he had become a close family friend, he did not want them to call him "mister". He enjoyed the visits and a chance to feel part of a big family, and he watched the children solicitously as they grew: especially the oldest girl, Anna. Not only was she pretty, but she had a pleasing disposition, as well. Above all, she was a straightforward child. When she made a mistake, she never tried to blame someone else or make excuses for herself. She was deeply religious and radiated a serenity that few girls her age possessed.

But when Anna was 19, her best girlfriend died, and she became deeply depressed. She withdrew from the family and seldom participated in the picnics or dances her brother, Hans, organized. Her parents worried because she became listless and started losing weight. She took lonely walks and often stayed in her room alone for hours at a time.

One day her sister Gertrude discovered Anna praying, and told the family. Their father, who had been a lieutenant general in the German cavalry, was a no-nonsense man who had little understanding for this kind of piety. The quickest, easiest solution to his problem seemed to be to find Anna a husband to take her mind off her grief. And who better than a family friend like Father? After all, there were three more daughters to marry off, and the hard-working Dutch-German businessman was a suitable partner.

Anna was called into the library where her parents and Father were having coffee. Her stern-faced father, never one to waste time or words, turned abruptly to her and said, "Anna, our friend here has asked for your hand in marriage."

She was flabbergasted. Never had it occurred to her that her father's friend, whom she considered to be an old man—after all, she was only 22 and he was 35—wanted her as a wife. She had the presence of mind to ask for a fortnight to make up her mind, but as soon as Father left, she told her parents she did not want to get married—to him or anyone else—she wanted to enter a convent.

"Nonsense! Crazy ideas!" her father roared. His mind was made up, and Anna and her mother had little to say in the matter. After two weeks of demands and refusals, Anna at last gave in and promised to marry the family friend. The wedding took place in July 1904, and they left immediately for Enken, where Father had started his own business. I have often wondered how the "almost nun" felt when within 11 years, she had given birth to eight children.

Enough now of dreaming about the past. I will need all of my strength to survive the all too present ordeal of my imprisonment. But, if I am to survive, I must remember the good days of the past.

They took my baby from me, though I screamed and cried and begged. My only comfort was that he was with my mother, and I knew she would take care of little Frans until I was free to do so myself. But when would I be free? What did they know, and how would they use it against me?

I was taken to a prison in Amsterdam on May 12, and placed in solitary confinement. It had been only a year since Dutch ears had first heard the thunder of Nazi artillery and bombs. Within a week, on a Friday, I was transported to the "pre-trial" prison at Nürnberg, Germany, where I encountered the 11 Ukrainian tag players.

The cell door opened suddenly and a guard stepped in. He spoke curtly to me, and as I slowly stood, the other women parted silently. The guard and I left the building and crossed the courtyard, which was the center of the four-building complex. An elevator took us to the fourth or fifth floor and we entered a sparsely furnished room. There were three chairs behind a table with a green felt cover: two were occupied by plain-clothed Gestapo; the guard who brought me sat in the empty one.

I stood during the entire interrogation. Over and over they asked me about my anti-Nazi activities, helping French prisoners of war, concealing Jewish babies, writing anti-Nazi "propaganda", hiding from the authorities. They seemed to know so much about my husband and me, and what we had been doing. I could hardly breathe, I was so frightened. Sweat broke out all over my body and I was sure the men could hear my heart pounding, it echoed so loudly in my ears.

But soon I realized they were quite vague in their questions, and I came to believe they were going only on the strength of suspicions. Each of the three men would ask me something, and often one would blurt out a second question before I could answer the first. They asked the same things repeatedly, then suddenly they would rephrase the words, or shout, trying to confuse me.

One of them stood and circled around me slowly. His fat face reflected superiority and cruelty.

"Why do you hesitate?" he asked in his whiny voice. "Why must you take so long to answer these simple questions? We need only to have the truth from you, and then we will release you."

I swallowed thickly, trying to bring moisture into my mouth and throat. "Because I know that in Germany, you can twist my words around to mean things that aren't true," I blurted out.

His face dropped in surprise. Then he struck me with his fist. The ring on his middle finger tore into my cheek. Blood rolled in a thin, hot stream from my nostril and I put my hand up to wipe it away—it tickled—and he hit me again.

The session continued for two hours, with their questions becoming more insistent, their insults more humiliating. I was struck in the face many times and the blood from my nose and the cuts on my face dried in meandering trails along my jaw and on the front and collar of my dress.

My eyes almost swollen shut, I was prodded and pushed back to my cell.

Within a few hours, the same guard came again for me, saying this time that I was going to see the doctor. I could hardly believe it, but I was very grateful. We went to the same building, only this time we went downstairs into the basement. I remember thinking to myself that it was an odd place for a doctor to have his office.

The room we entered looked like a big gymnasium, with metal apparatuses mounted at intervals along the walls. There were two men in white coats, and one of them motioned for me to be seated. I almost felt that I should make conversation with him, if he was the doctor who was going to treat my injuries, but his demeanor didn't encourage any of the social amenities. I sat on what looked like an old-fashioned doctor's scales, with the patient seated over the scales, and the balancing weights on a frame behind the patient's head. The doctor—for I assumed he was such—took my arms and placed them on the arms of the chair. My legs, which I had crossed, were moved so that my feet were flat on the floor.

Suddenly, I couldn't move. My forearms and thighs were encircled by metal clamps, pinning me to the chair, all at a flip of a switch by the second man, who now walked up behind me. He lowered a metal "fingered" contraption onto my head, and tightened it around my skull with screws that pulled at my hair and tore my scalp. Then, like a metronome setting the beat for a prelude to contrived terror, the head gear—and my head—started moving from side to side, slowly, horribly...left to right, right to left, tick, tock, tick...tock.

CHAPTER TWO

Saved by Recollections of my Childhood

To the side and up, to the side and up, my neck bent and then straightened obediently. If I closed my eyes, I became dizzy and nauseated, but if I left them open, I had to take in all that was going on in the room as they tortured other prisoners. They stopped the machine to feed me—and I got good food. They stopped it when I said I needed the bathroom. And they stopped it to take me into the interrogation room. It took some time, but slowly I was able to reduce my awareness, both physical and mental, and systematically, I filed away the horrors I was confronted with hour after hour, and closed the doors in my mind behind them.

My second day in the "doctor's office", one of the interrogators unfastened my dress and lowered it to my waist. Then he inserted long, thin needles into the nipples of my breasts. All of my strength went into keeping myself from telling them what they wanted to hear. My front teeth ground through my lower lip and I gagged on the dull metallic taste of my own blood. In my mind, I screamed a confession and bellowed out the names of every underground resistance worker I knew. But somehow, all the sound stayed inside me. My struggle with the piercing agony remained a silent one. Yet each time they began to unfasten my dress panic filled me again and I prayed wordlessly that I would never speak out loud. Knowing what was coming, the anticipation was almost worse than the actual pain.

I was convinced by then that the Gestapo was sure of nothing, and that encouraged me to hold on. I could "think" much of the pain away, most easily by making myself terribly angry. All I had to do was watch the young men as they ran through a series of tortures daily, like small children given new, destructive toys and dispensable doll bodies, with a parental go-ahead that sanctioned and rewarded whatever games they could invent.

All around me were people going through the same pain and indignities I was subjected to, and although I knew none of them, I experienced a heavy suffering in realizing I could do nothing to help them. One young man died in the interrogation room after they had tortured and beaten him, his screams flooding into the main room through the half-open doors until at last his throat was too dry and raw, his lungs too weak to fill with air. Moments after the violent cries had faded, his persecutors pushed their way through the double doors, dragging his body between them, his bloody, shapeless head sliding and bumping on the tile floor as they pulled him across the room by his heels.

One Gestapo—the perfect Aryan with blonde hair, blue eyes and a handsome, intelligent face—questioned a French woman. She, too, had her dress pulled down around her waist. The man smoked a cigarette as he asked her a number of questions, and he picked up one of her hands, saying, "You French women have such beautiful, elegant hands." Then he took his cigarette and burned each of her fingertips, smiling as he did so.

On another day, they tortured a five-year-old girl in front of her mother. They demanded to know where the woman's "Communist swine" of a husband was, but she could tell them nothing. I closed my eyes and prayed that my own child was safe from harm and that I would soon be with him. As hours dragged by and fear became a constant, almost physical companion, I drew more and more on my memories, willing myself away through the stone walls of my hell to the green, free countryside of a pre-Hitler Germany.

Two months before I was born in June 1915, my father died of cancer, leaving my German mother at the age of 34 in a foreign country with seven children to care for and another on the way. There was also the clothing business, which he had always run by himself, and which she knew nothing about, not to mention the Dutch way of marketing.

Then her mother, who had earlier suffered a stroke, also died. Although her doctor strongly advised against it, Mother felt she must make the long journey from Holland to her home in East Prussia, and when I was six weeks old, she took me with her to visit her father, the old count. He persuaded her to leave me with him, while she returned to her seven other children in Holland.

I've been told it took me a long time to learn to talk. The easy words like "Papa" and "Mamma" had no meaning for me since my father was dead and my mother was far away in another country. The German word for grandfather—Grossvater—is quite a difficult word for a small child. One day in the library, Grossvater took me on his lap and tried to make me say "danke"—thank you. As he repeated it louder and louder and bent closer to me, I watched him curiously. When he was close enough, I reached up and pulled his mustache. The word he cried out was not one I was supposed to learn. He put me down and I trotted over to my turtle, which was lying in the corner. It had pulled in its head and legs, and I tried to get them back out. As I saw it was hopeless, I pushed the stubborn thing and said, "Du bist dumm", which means, "You are dumb".

When Grossvater heard this, he hastened to pick me up and praise me. I stuck my finger in his cheek and repeated, "Du bist dumm." Grossvater agreed, "Sure, I am dumb, sweetheart." After that, I caught up with my speaking ability and learned a lot of words that Mother would certainly not have approved of.

Grossvater was for me father, mother, playmate—everything. My first six years of life were spent in the greatest of freedom; and though he was a strange man with some outrageous ideas, I loved him dearly. He brought me up as a boy, referring to himself and me, as "We guys", and it was my early training in all the boyhood pursuits like bow hunting and trap making that saved my life later. The woods and fields of Grossvater's estate were filled with mice and squirrels that succumbed to my child-size bow and arrows, and I lay for hours at a time watching my traps to see just how the rabbit approached the bait and how quickly prey was snared. A simple change in the lure and placement of the snare resulted in the entrapment of troublesome birds that raided Grossvater's crops. When I was four years old, my mother sent a doll for my birthday. Grossvater opened the parcel, picked the doll up by one leg as if it were a dirty thing, and threw it out the window, saying, "I'll give you some white mice to play with."

And so he did, in addition to a whole menagerie of other pets which Grossvater gave "easy" names, like Bonifacius Turtle, Nebuchadnezzar Squirrel, Nicodemus Hamster and the Mouse family of Zacharias, Zebedues, Judocus, and so on. Only my dog had a simple name—Heikko. All these animals populated my little world and Grossvater talked about them as if they were human playmates. If I did something wrong, he might say, "Look at Bonifacius, he does not approve of your behavior at all," and I would feel so ashamed, and would ask the turtle to forgive me and forget what I had done.

I was brought up by men because all the servants were ex-soldiers from Grossvater's old cavalry regiment, except for one old maid, who made herself scarce whenever possible. I learned to climb trees, jump over ditches with a pole, and made my own bow and arrows. On my fifth birthday, I got a horse, Roland, and learned to ride. I also got a baby chick. One of the hens was hatching and I had been promised a chick of my own if the eggs hatched before my birthday. Luckily, the babies made their appearance the afternoon before. Every spring I got a lamb, complete with blue ribbon and bell. When it grew up, the lamb joined the rest of the herd, but I believed it had run away, and when a new one was brought to me the next spring, wearing the same ribbon and bell, I was sure it was my errant pet, just as I was confident that my breakfast egg came from my very own chicken.

After I turned five, I acquired a tutor. Mother had extracted a promise from Grossvater that I would come home to Holland at age six to start school. I didn't know one word of Dutch, and Grossvater also wanted to prepare me in subjects like religion, arithmetic, spelling and writing. Old Dr. Schultz was a retired schoolteacher who welcomed the opportunity to supplement his meager pension. It was winter when he arrived, and we were installed in the library. He had hardly been there an hour the first day when Joseph, Grossvater's valet, came to tell Dr. Schultz that there was a telephone call for him. At that time, we had only one instrument in the whole house, and it was near the pantry. As soon as the old man had left the room, somebody threw a snowball against the window. I climbed up on the bench beneath the windowsill to look out. There was Grossvater with my coat, cap and mittens. "Open the window and come out. I'll catch you. It is much too beautiful out here for anyone to sit in a stuffy room."

I was too delighted with Grossvater's gay mood to ask myself why he made me play hooky after first hiring a tutor for me. Poor old Dr. Schulz never understood why the phone had gone dead by the time he reached it.

I don't know for sure how long they tortured me, but I believe it was for just over a week. Eight days and eight nights of the side-to-side motion, interrupted only occasionally. There were other things they did to me, more creative forms of torture that just to think of made me curl into the fetal position and fight to blank out the pictures in my head, but I cannot bring myself to reveal those things here.

On the ninth day, I was taken to another building in the same complex. There was a woman guard. I remember her name was Frau Arnold, and she said, "You come from the Gestapo? Oh, you poor girl." The guards were civilians, and didn't necessarily endorse the Fuhrer's policies as commands from God, as did so many of the Gestapo and SS.

We went into a shower room, and I was so weak I could hardly stand. Finally, she steadied me and kept me upright beneath the spray of clear water. My strength was draining rapidly from me, now that the ordeal of the doctor's office was over, and I was ready to collapse. But, I shuddered to think of the filth on my skin, the stench of my body, and I longed for warmth and cleansing. It was to be my last warm bath for a full year.

I dream of former days...

Grossvater and I walked each morning after breakfast if the weather was clear: he, to check on the workers in the fields and I, to survey my little realm of worshippers—animal and human alike—and to beg for more of Grossvater's fascinating stories.

Even though we started our stroll early, the field workers would have already put in half a day's labor. Grossvater would sometimes point to one of them and say, "See that fellow there? You have to have a lot of respect for him. He earns his living, while I just lay about." He was interested in every aspect of the work on the estate, which encompassed about 2000 acres, part of it forest.

One day as we were returning home, he told me it was time to go in, but I was feeling rather self-important and informed him that I had first to go to the little pavilion to visit my animals, and that I wasn't about to go back to the house until I had done so. An argument ensued and I chose to throw a tantrum. In order to be sure I had his attention, I threw myself into one of 16 water ponds that had been dug around the estate. The water wasn't deep, so I could hardly drown, which we both knew.

"So, now you can learn to swim," was all Grossvater said, and strolled calmly off in the direction of home. The drama was wasted and I hurriedly waded out of the pond, leaving small footprints of mud, water and moss as I sheepishly trotted after him. At the door, he turned and said, "Take off your clothes and dry them here on the lawn", and that was the end of the tantrum for me.

Frau Arnold let me go to bed, although it was the middle of the day. These cells had a bed and table that folded up into the wall, and under ordinary circumstances, the beds were to be put up immediately after the prisoners awoke in the morning, for there was to be no idle sitting on the beds, nor sleeping in, even when there was nothing else to do.

I slept. For a day, two days, I don't know. But they must have kept close watch on me, for when I finally awakened, it was only minutes before someone came in with food. My dream was over.

I was alone, as I had not been in the cell across the green. The four months I spent there in solitary confinement were to be the best of all the time I spent as a prisoner. Far from being a punishment, time spent alone was vastly sweeter than the days and nights of no privacy or silence at all.

It was clean there, too. Each prisoner was required to clean her own cell, including buffing the floor with a wool rag. The entire building had parquet floors, and in the hallway, two Russian girls were made to buff the floor each day. Well-matched in strength and height, like a pair of work horses the girls moved back and forth, to and fro, for hours. A box full of stones was placed on a wool blanket, and they had to pull the heavy load through the corridor, leaning into the chain that crossed their chests. The pressure and movement of the wool gave the floors a glossy shine.

In addition to cleaning, each prisoner had to work during the day. I spent hours putting paper labels on crayons. A piece of hard cardboard was placed in front of each worker. A remnant of cloth was attached to that. I moistened the sticky side of the little labels, separating them and laying them out on the sheet in front of me. The crayons went on top of the labels—sorted by color— and then a swift hand movement rolled the crayons up in their labels all at once. Everyone tried to master the most efficient method of labeling, because if a prisoner failed to fill a daily quota of banded crayons, the food ration—which was already little enough—would be cut.

Everything in prison revolved around food: it was used in a punishment/reward system; the day was figured in hours-since and hours-until meals. We longed for even the smallest amount more than we were getting. So many of my thoughts were only on food. We didn't get enough to live on, and yet it was too much to allow us to starve to death.

As a child...

Grossvater grew wheat in the summertime, and it stretched so high that I could hide in it, only giving my location away by giggling as I thought of Grossvater searching and searching for his "lost guy", and as I listened to his heartbroken pleas and gruff demands to know where I was. Most of our food was grown on the estate, too, like potatoes, vegetables and fruit. The dairy workers brought in gallons of warm, sudsy-looking cow's milk that became our butter and cheese, and I can still conjure up the acrid taste of buttermilk from the icehouse, and the feel of my throat closing on the thick, lumpy drink.

We also slaughtered steers, calves, pigs and fowl to be smoked and treated and put away for a year's use. An old woman named Mille took care of the chickens, ducks, geese, swans and peacocks that provided a cacophony of early morning greetings and a kaleidoscope of colored feathers.

Mille had only two teeth left in her mouth, and she was an alcoholic. Grossvater had warned her: "What you do in your free time is none of my business, but during working hours, I won't tolerate any drinking."

She made her own brew of cherries, strawberries and raspberries, and kept a whole row of wide glass bottles on a shelf in her little house. One summer day as she was cleaning, she poured the berry residue out her window. The chickens eating bugs in the flowerbed below were greatly surprised but thoroughly pleased with this unexpected treat, and in no time at all, the usually sedate and proper old hens were cackling loud, staggering around, and falling over each other. A crowd gathered as word spread among the nearby workers, and they all laughed hard. Suddenly, Grossvater walked into their midst, a curious smile on his face, and the laughter died. Everyone knew Mille had been warned and threatened. Grossvater's smile faded, and he chewed his lip seriously as the hens, oblivious to authority, continued their drunken chatter. Grossvater pulled a big handkerchief from the breast pocket of his old jacket, blew his nose loudly and walked away without speaking. Running after him, I could see his great shoulders heaving up and down with suppressed laughter.

Having led a straight-backed military life for so many years, Grossvater began to mellow as he aged, perhaps because of my young company. My mother sometimes found it hard to believe the stories I told her of my adventures with Grossvater, because she knew him only as the stern disciplinarian who would not tolerate such nonsense as her "excessive" piety, and who made every decision in his smoothly run castle, from what they would eat to whom his children would marry.

Grossvater poured out his love on me as if he were making up for lost time and trying to offer amends, through me, to those loved ones who never glimpsed his concern and affection through this rugged exterior. I could have almost anything I asked for, do anything I wanted to do, and if he had been even a little less strong in character, he could well have turned me into an unruly monster. But, luckily for both of us, he could revert to the role of taskmaster as it was called for due to my lapses in manners.

I discovered the cherry orchard one summer, and Grossvater warned me not to pick any cherries until they were ripe. But they looked so good, and I was sure no harm could come from pilfering a handful of shiny, blushing beauties, so I shinnied up a tree and started munching. The more I ate, the more I wanted, and I took great delight in spitting the pits at various targets on the ground below my perch. But then I began to feel very full, and soon the full feeling turned to a suspicion that I had somehow stuffed myself with sharp, heavy rocks. I could hardly make my way down the trunk of the tree, holding my stomach with one hand as I had to, to keep myself from exploding. But down I came, and made a mad dash around the corner of a barn.

Up came the cherries, hot and tangy. I thought the urge to retch would never stop, and I began to cry and sob, curling up on the ground and wondering whether Grossvater would be able to get along without me now that I was dying, and hoping he would never discover what had caused my sudden demise.

I opened my eyes at the sound of footsteps and saw Grossvater leaning against the corner of the building. He looked at me, the mess on the ground, and out to the orchard.

"Aha, I understand," he said grimly. Pointing his cane to the tower room, which was mine, he told me to go up there and stay.

Saved by Recollections of my Childhood 23

For three days, I was so sick I became convinced that I was indeed on my deathbed. Grossvater sent the doctor, but my beloved companion did not come himself, and guilt and misery added to my suffering.

When I was allowed to get up, Grossvater sent for me. His favorite chair stood in the library next to the fireplace, which was across the room from the door. It was a large room, and as a rule, I would run straight through it and hop up onto his lap. Now, with my bad conscience, it took a very, very long time to reach him. He was reading and pretended not to see me. After a few minutes, he put down his book, took off his reading glasses, and looked at my fearful, begging face. To my horror, he started laughing.

"Aren't you the one who climbed the cherry tree? Didn't you eat the sour cherries? Well, how did they taste? Would you like some more?"

I stood there, feeling ten inches high, trying to swallow the hurt in the top of my throat and hold back the hot, flowing tears. Then Grossvater picked me up and held me tight, rocking me back and forth as I promised to be good, oh, so good.

The Nationalsozialistische Deutsche Arbeiterpartei (NSDAP or Nazi Party) won the Lippe elections in January 1933 and Adolf Hitler, the Austrian rabble-rouser, was made Chancellor of Germany. A book burning in May was aimed at ridding the country of any material that was "subversive or potentially damaging to the root of German thought and the German home"—especially any written by Jews. The first of a series of plots to overthrow the Party was discovered in June, resulting in the arrest of Ernst Roehm, head of the Sturm Abteilung—Storm Department, also referred to as Brown Shirts—and a roundup of SA leaders and troops amid rumors of homosexuality. A proclamation in July limited bearing arms to soldiers only. Hindenburg died the next month, and Hitler was made Reich's Chancellor. An August election showed 90 percent of the German voters supporting Hitler as President.

The timing was perfect for a commanding, determined leader like Hitler. Germany had been defeated in a major war (World War I) and a harsh peace treaty (Treaty of Versailles) brought her to her knees. Industry was curtailed and historic national boundaries shrunk. Devastating inflation and mass unemployment had Germans standing in soup lines that stretched for blocks. Communism and anarchy increased daily. And then along came a little man with a big voice who promised salvation and showed immediate results. Construction of the Autobahn and the Volkswagen (People's Car) factory put thousands back to work, and food on their tables.

In 1935, the Nürnberg Laws had deprived Jews of German citizenship and the right to own real estate. Hitler didn't invent anti-Semitism; he only revived and encouraged it. The Nazi Party needed a racial enemy to unite its members in a "cause of the heart", and Hitler ignited a national flame of hatred for the people he said had been "involved in every form of human corruption, betrayed Germany in the war, had control of banks and foreign capital, had dominance in Bolshevism." Very few bothered to examine the incongruities of the claims. Those who protested were the ones who were wrong. A Communist uprising resulted in mass arrests, and thousands were incarcerated in concentration camps.

The signs proclaiming "Juden verboten" and "Juden unerwünscht" that usually kept Jews in their places were removed from store and restaurant windows during the 1936 Olympics in Berlin, to show foreign visitors and press that persecution of the Jews was only so much nasty gossip. The "superior" Germans swept the field and captured 33 gold, 26 silver and 30 bronze medals, but Hitler's dream of superiority snagged when the Americans refused to salute the Third Reich by dipping their colors on parade. And Hitler left the stand rather than shake hands with Jesse Owens, the American black man who took the gold in four track and field events.

Fall Rot—Case Red—swung into action as Germany prepared a two-front war against England and Poland in 1937. At the Paris Embassy in November 1938, a Jew shot the German Third Secretary. Jewish homes and businesses were vandalized, and Jews were beaten in reprisal on the "night of breaking glass"—Kristallnacht. British Prime Minister-Chamberlain gave Poland an unconditional guarantee of military assistance a few weeks before Hitler's 50th birthday in April 1939. The headlines of the Völkischer Beobachter—People's Observer—in late August read: "Whole of Poland in War Fever! 1,500,000 Men Mobilized! Uninterrupted Troop Transport Toward the Frontier".

Holland's troops were mobilized August 29 and England declared war on Germany September 3. Hitler's offer of peace was turned down the next month. A bomb intended for him injured

Saved by Recollections of my Childhood 25

several others in November. And Russia invaded Finland, resulting in a peace treaty in March 1940.

Germany attacked and defeated Holland in May. Belgium surrendered the same month, and the Wehrmacht entered Paris in mid-June. An armistice with France was signed the next week, and England refused Hitler's second offer of negotiated peace in July. The next month, Berlin was bombed. His eye on Russia, Hitler had asked his aides for an attack analysis as early as mid-1940, even as Stalin was supplying war materials, including oil, to Germany. A non-aggression pact between the two nations was ignored as Hitler lunged eastward to acquire Lebensraum—living space for the expansion of the Aryan race.

It was the summer of 1941 and America had yet to officially enter the war. The crack of artillery and the drone of bomber engines heralded daybreak on June 22, 1941 as Nazi troops penetrated Russia's western paunch, opening up another Front and dramatically weakening the Nazi threat.

The wail of the siren and the rush of guards in the hall warned me before I heard the bombers: air raid! All around me, prisoners began hammering on the doors of their cells, yelling and cursing at the guards to let them out. The fear and excitement caught me and I added my voice to theirs. Suddenly, the corridor was empty and the only noise was our own shouts and the increasing roar in the skies. It came to each of us at almost the same time, because the yelling died out and there was a moment of eerie quiet as it registered: the guards were in the bomb shelter, explosions were jarring the foundations of the prison, and we were all locked, helpless, in our second and third floor cells.

An agonized scream of panic swelled, and the frantic yelling and frenzied pounding began again. I kicked at the door and struck it with my fists, crying and praying. Each breath burst from my lungs and sweat ran down the sides of my face. My God, is it all to end like this? Have I survived the pain and indignity of Nazi torture only to be killed by English bombs? Oh, God, where are You? How can You let me go through this alone? Mama, mama, mama. God let me out of here. Let me go home. I want to go home. I am sorry for whatever it was that I did to deserve this hell. Please. Please. Stop the noise, stop the bombs, stop the planes. Let me live and be free or let me die right here.

That night, my sobs lapsed into whimpers and sighs, as I lay alone in the silent prison cell. I told myself I should be thankful that none of the bombs had found the complex, but my spirits were too low. I was ready to give up, almost wishing the prison had been destroyed, and me along with it. I had suffered enough. I could accept no more. I was tired and heartsick, hungry and lonely. I could not take another step without help.

Acknowledging my miserable loneliness brought on new tears, and my body shook as I let myself sink further into despair, almost not caring enough to keep filling my lungs with air. Then my tears were spent and my tired brain stalled and refused to focus on any more of the horrors I had been mentally putting myself through. I reached out my hand into the darkness and said aloud, "My Lord, it is up to you. I can't go on alone."

I felt a presence at that time, an almost physical reassurance, like a hand grasping mine. The burden that had weighed so heavily on me was gone. At last, as I allowed myself to weaken and give up my one-woman battle against what was happening to me; I also let in a power that had been there all along. I had cried out for His help so many times, yet I had steeled myself and trudged on as soon as the prayer was uttered, without looking back at the helping hand that had stretched out towards me.

And so it was that I found Jesus Christ—in solitary confinement.

CHAPTER THREE

Condemned to Rothenfeld Prison

My trial was in September and I was convicted of falsification of documents—they had caught me with my "Laura Carp" identification papers and passport. I was sentenced to 10 months in prison, with credit for time already served, and would be transferred to another prison, since Nürnberg was for pre-trial prisoners only. But I had to wait until a large group of prisoners was assembled for transport.

That evening, I was put into a cell with a 23-year-old woman named Liesl who had been condemned to death. She had stolen from hotels and Nazi officers, impersonated a baroness, neglected her illegitimate child, and infected certain high-ranking officials with venereal disease. Volksschädling, they called her—a public threat. Liesl began to tell me what awaited her, as she had been told by other prisoners. The night before the execution, she would have a meal of whatever she asked for. This I doubted seriously, because food was in short supply all over Germany, and I couldn't see the Nazis wasting good food on a woman who was going to die the next day. In the morning, she continued, they would cut her hair off short and give her a low-necked blouse to wear. Then she would be taken to another room where she would lie down on a table and her arms and legs would be strapped down. The table would move, the blade would fall, and her head would tumble into a basket of wood shavings.

I stared at her in horror, not knowing what to say, thinking: here is a girl only three years younger than I am, and by the end of the week, she will be dead. The decapitation scene flashed garishly before me. And then, as if she hadn't spoken before, Liesl began calmly reciting the story again; from what she'd eat for dinner to the ingenious way her head would drop right into the basket. Late into the night, she repeated the tale over and over with a dreadful fascination for detail, and I thought it must be her only means of self-control, her pitiful attempt at not admitting that after the knife dropped, she would be dead. Since that night, I have been decapitated in my dreams many times.

Next, I came to a cell with three other women, and I began to realize what I was going to be exposed to in the next few months. I was in prison. These people were criminals. I could not believe my naivety. One cellmate was a thief, a postal worker who had been stealing food packages that were sent to German families by their soldier-relatives on the Front. Any country had more food then than Germany did, and the men sent gifts of perfume, cognac and silk stockings, as well. The other two cellmates had been convicted, I learned to my horror, of killing their newborn children. After the tragedy I had suffered in being so abruptly separated from my own little Frans, I had neither understanding nor empathy for these two animals. I recoiled in disgust if they even came near me, for they were vile, demented creatures in my eyes, and the thought of even touching something they may have brushed against or breathing the same air, made me sick to my stomach. I was determined to get away from them, but how?

Each morning, the prisoners were taken outside to the courtyard and made to march briskly. This was done in an orderly, controlled fashion as all German procedures were carried out. The marching prisoners soon took on the uniformity and stiff appearance of trained soldiers, and corners were executed smartly. My desire to get away from the women in my cell, and to keep away from others, who would perhaps be worse, would get no satisfaction through normal channels. I had to risk something more daring. As we marched in formation, I broke out in song, yelling the Dutch words at the clouds in the sky:

> *"It is the duty of every boy to give his utmost power for the independence of his beloved Fatherland. Hurray! Hurray! For the Netherlands, hurray! For queen and Fatherland, every boy is on guard."*

My arms swished stiffly from next to my leg, up in an arc until they brushed my ears, then down again, as I bounded out of line, my high-stepping legs almost crashing my knees into my chest. The looks of surprise and disbelief on the faces of guards and prisoners alike were so funny that I almost broke out in laughter, which would have been fatal. Nobody in his or her right mind would do what I had done, much less admit it was planned. Quickly, the guards subdued me and rushed everyone back inside. After a short consultation among themselves, they hustled me down the stairs and into an empty cell in the unused basement. They thought something in my mind had finally snapped, that I had gone over the edge, so I was treated like a potentially violent maniac. But I had my privacy again away from the baby killers and I was, in my silent room, as safe from English bombs as I could get.

And then my thoughts drifted back to my youth. My idyllic existence with Grossvater ended when I was six years old. Mother and my seven brothers and sisters came to the castle for a month-long visit and when they left, I went with them. Mother had brought me a white dress—my first feminine apparel. Two of my brothers, jealous of my established status at the castle, began to torment me the moment I appeared in the uncomfortable, scratchy garment. I could only take so much of their exaggerated exclamations over my beauty. I ran angrily from the house and flung myself, starched dress and all, into the nearest pond.

That was the first time I got a spanking. Grossvater had never touched me in anger, or as punishment, but Mother didn't hesitate a single moment. It was then that I realized how drastically my world was about to change. For six years, I had been an only child, cared for by a doting guardian. Now I was just the youngest of eight, forced to share and wait my turn.

My mother was strict and incapable, at least at that time, of showing any emotion. She never raised her voice when she was angry, yet she never laughed when she was amused. She spoke always in a soft voice, sat straight in her chair, and was in constant control of all her movements. She had an extra strong sense of duty and propriety. When I was older, I asked her one day if it had seemed impossible for her to carry on after my father's death, with eight children to raise by herself and a business to conduct in a man's world. She looked at me blankly for a moment, and then said matter-of-factly, "Nobody asked me if I could or wanted to. I had to do it, so I did."

The nine of us lived frugally, but Mother gave generously to charity. There was famine in Germany, Austria and Hungary during the post-World War era, and a priest in our hometown arranged for groups of 50-60 children to be imported and hosted by local Catholic families. We had 10 of them in our home during a period of a few years, sometimes two at the same time. They usually stayed three to four months, got lots of meat, milk and eggs, and when they left, Mother gave each of them a suitcase full of clothing. When I first arrived in Holland, a boy from Dusseldorf came to stay with us. His name was Harry and he was my first love. With Harry, I could talk German and tell about my "other life," the years I spent with Grossvater, so when it came time for him to leave, I was desperate. He was my only friend and my one true love. If Harry was leaving, I would simply have to go with him. That was out of the question, Mother said. Harry had to go and I had to stay. At least let me see him off at the train station, I pleaded tearfully.

"Oh, no," Mother argued. "We've already seen one tantrum here in this house. Let's not make fools of ourselves in public." Mother was determined, but so was I. At last, she promised me a bar of chocolate if I would stay home. Never! My oldest sister offered another bar. How dare she? Finally, Harry himself begged me not to come, and offered another bribe. So, for three chocolate bars, I swallowed my pride and denied my true love.

Life in a small town where everybody knew us wasn't easy for me. Just as a wild bird shouldn't be kept in a cage, a child who has been brought up in freedom shouldn't be suddenly restricted to an opposite way of life. We were never allowed to play outside, our house had neither lawn nor garden. We had to come straight home from school, and mustn't make any noise that could be heard by the customers on the ground floor. The second and third floors were our living quarters and the fourth floor contained a stock room and tailor shop. I was forbidden to visit the fourth floor because Mother was afraid I'd be up to no good.

But the tailors loved music and I loved to sing, so we established a friendly agreement. Two songs brought one penny: a German song alone, one penny: German song with gestures like rocking a baby or smoking a pipe, two pennies. Sometimes I sang and sang until they paid me to shut up. And when they sent me to the grocery store to buy chocolate each of them gave me half of their candy bar.

At night, a man came with a hooked stick that pulled a little chain on the gas street lamps, igniting the gas and lighting the streets for safety. I decided one night to shut off all the lamps on our street, and as soon as he disappeared around the corner, I climbed the lampposts and extinguished the flames. The merchants on our street complained to the gas company, and the poor man had to come back and relight the lamps. As soon as he left, I snuffed the lights out again. This went on for quite some time, and I was thoroughly enjoying the game until he caught on. He waited around the corner, and then ran out to grab me as I was halfway up a pole. A passing patrolman took me to the police station at the lamp lighter's request. I was locked inside a closet until Mother came for me. Being so well known, she was quite embarrassed, and I suffered the consequences.

Another time, I put firecrackers on the tracks where the horse-drawn streetcar ran. The horse spooked and ran; the people panicked. I landed in the police station again. It didn't take long to establish a reputation in town as a mischievous prankster, and "decent" people warned their children not to play with me. I know now that I caused my poor mother a lot of grief in my misguided quest for attention. She often looked at me with a puzzled expression in her eyes, much like, I'm sure, a poor old hen that had hatched a duck's egg and couldn't understand why her offspring wouldn't stay away from the river. And every time she turned her back or relaxed her vigil, in I would go, flailing my wings and covering her with water.

Before Hitler came to power, Germany suffered inflation after inflation. In the morning, you might be a millionaire, but that evening, your millions could only buy a loaf of bread. You could post a letter for a million bucks. Unemployment was so high that former professors were lucky to find jobs as street sweepers. One government followed another. A nation of hard working, proud people groveled in confusion, never sure of the next meal. Germany's colonies had been taken away, and along her former borders, Germans now lived under Polish or Czech rule. I think the most dangerous man of that time, even more so than Hitler, was Josef Goebbels, Propaganda Minister, because he knew exactly what would work to unite the German people behind a cause, in this instance, Nazism. The Germans love to march, and Goebbels gave them marching songs. School children were brought into the streets every morning, marching and singing, and waving the banners of the Third Reich. Every boy loves to play with guns, and Goebbels provided shooting ranges and instructors. They were drilled like soldiers, those tiny, innocent children, and they thrived on it. A German in a uniform thinks he's a big shot, and Goebbels supplied the uniforms.

It didn't take them long to learn. Ideologies were pumped into them by the hour. The Hitler Jugend (Hitler Youth) sponsored picnics and outings, patriotic fun, they called it, for the young boys and girls. All they had to do was choose between a day in the fresh country air singing songs and playing games, or a day in a hot, stuffy church, since the activities began Sunday mornings.

"We had to belong to the Hitler Jugend," I hear Germans say now, 40 years later, "That's not so." It was just easier to join than to risk harassment. If you weren't a Nazi Party member, and you taught school, for example, you'd lose your job. Independent businessmen suffered from not being Nazis. The Party would let it be known, sometimes through a newspaper, that you weren't a member, and if anyone still dared to patronize your shop, they would be stopped and asked, "Are you going to do business with someone who is against our Führer?"

Nazism was like a disease. Everything, everybody, was affected. The ones who were against Hitler were very few, and even those who didn't approve of his methods were too afraid to be actively against him. They became Party members to save their jobs or businesses, or just to be going with the crowd. One of my aunts and her husband owned a wholesale grain business in Germany. They weren't Nazis, and refused to join the Party. Subsequently, they lost everything, and he ended up delivering milk. Their oldest daughter, a nun now, was a very religious girl who went to church every morning. One day, as she walked home from church with a prayer book in her hand, a Party member took a picture of her. A Nazi bulletin board had been attached to a wall of her father's big warehouse, and the photograph soon appeared there, entitled Pfaffenbraut (priests' bride).

The Catholic Church was a major enemy of the Nazis, and so they directed a campaign of slander against the church, centered on scandals over homosexuality in orphanages or boarding schools. The Nazis made these isolated cases known through their newspapers, accusing priests and nuns of demoralizing Germany's youth. I was in Germany studying at the University at Breslau then, so I was able to research the incidents. I found that neither nuns nor priests were involved, but lay teachers, who were dismissed as soon as their practices were discovered.

I started writing articles, exposing the truth about Nazism, and smuggled them out of Germany to be published in Holland. I didn't send the letters directly from Breslau, but mailed them to my mother's brother, who lived near the Dutch border. At that time, 1937, travel between Germany and Holland was not restricted, and he took them to Holland on regular business trips.

When I first came to Breslau, I had to find a family I could live with while I attended the university. There were no dormitories as there are on American campuses. And they had to be people I could trust, someone who wouldn't repeat every word I uttered, or spy on me. I met students who had been there the year before, and they told me about professors, mostly Jews, who had been dismissed from the university. Students were now required to sign a paper declaring loyalty to the government, or they could not study there. Being a foreigner, I wasn't made to do so. I was told many strange things, and I wondered sometimes if they were telling me just to see my reaction. There was an atmosphere of distrust over everything. Once some of us were sitting together when another student came into the room and said, "Heil, Hitler!" One of the young men said, "So what?" meaning it as a joke. The newcomer marched smartly over to the boy's chair and asked threateningly, "You dare to make a joke out of the name of our Führer?" The student backed down immediately.

Sometimes jokes were told about Hitler, but you never dared laugh, because you didn't know if the person who told the joke was being funny or if he was a Party member checking your allegiance to the Third Reich. Because Hitler promised an end to bad times, most students were quite supportive of the Party. There were student demonstrations, especially night torch parades, and their enthusiasm was scary. They weren't themselves. The cool, collected scholars of the day became hysterical chanters at the eerie flame-lit rallies.

There were a few whom I had identified as anti-Nazi. You soon noticed if their enthusiasm was real when the Party was discussed, and they always found an excuse for not participating in the torch parades. At the university, there were several study rooms for students who lived in quarters where they couldn't study easily. Many of them lived in houses that lacked good heating, and the study rooms were much warmer. There was adequate heating in the room I rented, but I still sometimes used the study quarters. It was there that I was first approached by a member of the underground.

A young man, one of the top students, very quiet and mature for his age, came up to me one day and asked me to go for a walk with him. We walked a long time, chatting about school and our interests, but it was not until we had left the city limits that he began to discuss politics and the situation in Germany. I was a little bit scared and didn't know how to answer him. I had no way of knowing whether he was really anti-Nazi. Still, he could tell I wasn't at all enthusiastic about the Nazi movement. "I'm a foreigner," I told him. "You can't expect me to feel the same as you Germans do." He smiled wistfully and said, "You must know, all Germans do not feel the same."

A few days after that, he caught up with me at school and asked if I'd like to go for a bike ride. We spent more and more time together, developing a special, though unromantic, relationship. Slowly, I began to reveal my strong feelings about Nazism as I came to trust him more. I knew by that time that he was seriously against the Party, and some of the remarks he made frightened me, for they could have meant his death if he were overheard.

"I loved Germany and its people more than Holland and the Dutch," I told him as I repeated the stories of my joyful childhood in East Prussia. "But when I came back to Germany in 1933, it had drastically changed, as my feelings have."

I had visited Grossvater's estate before my studies began that fall, expecting it to be the same as when I had last been there six years earlier. But everything had changed. The people were hesitant to talk, even to me, and didn't dare express an opinion on anything but the most casual subject. Friends and neighbors had been arrested for saying the wrong things, they told me. For example, one of the older servants had a nephew who had joined the Nazi Party. One evening a group of them sat talking when this young man, who had just been to a Party meeting and was still in uniform, joined them. The conversation was about war, and what would happen if Germany got involved again. The nephew expressed his opinion, but his uncle disagreed with him, saying, "What do you know, snotty nose, about war? You weren't even born during the last one!" The next day, the Gestapo—Geheime Staatspolizei or Secret State Police—

arrested the old man and sent him to a concentration camp. They said he had insulted the uniform.

My cousin, who had managed the estate for me since Grossvater's death, left Germany for Switzerland soon after I enrolled at the university, taking all the estate money with him to a Swiss bank, and I'm glad he did. I had been in school only three months when the Party confiscated the estate. The Gestapo said Grossvater had given German property to a foreigner, I had Dutch nationality, and that was not acceptable. I was allowed to take some of the furniture, but I couldn't use much at the time since I was living in a boarding house. The castle and grounds were given to the Hitler Jugend for use as a boys' summer camp.

Taking leave of all the people whom I had known for so many years was terribly hard for me. They all cried when we said goodbye, and invited me to come stay with them during my school vacations. I very rarely did that though, because I couldn't bear to see what had happened to Grossvater's house and grounds. The boys who spent their vacations there used the crystal chandelier in the hall as a target for their slingshots. The exquisite tapestries were torn from the walls, and buildings and gardens alike suffered from a battering by children who couldn't have cared less about the historical beauty of Grossvater's home.

After a year or so of increasingly more serious discussions about the Nazis, my friend confided in me that he belonged to a group of underground workers, people who were well aware of the threat of Nazism and determined to do as much as they could for the persecuted, even at the risk of their own lives. Some of the people the group helped were the professors who had been dismissed from the university and now were in financial straits and worried about the safety of their families. Some professors had simply disappeared, probably to concentration camps, but nobody knew for sure, or where. Members of the group came from all walks of life: students, priests, ministers, a doctor, and even a professor who was still employed at the university. We had meetings where we would talk and give each other moral support. Trepidation gnawed at each of us during the day and we soaked up every moment of companionship available to us. You seldom saw smiling people in the streets. Even when they marched and sang, the people didn't show happiness, just fanatic enthusiasm. Each day, we expected all hell to break loose, and we worked frantically to get as much done as we could.

There was one doctor who treated anyone who couldn't go to Party doctors. The Jews kept much to themselves, even before Hitler came to power, and they tended to patronize medical professionals of their own faith. By then, however, Jewish doctors were forbidden to practice, so this doctor treated Jewish patients at night in a rented room in the house of friends he knew to be anti-Nazi. He wasn't sure he could trust his nurse to keep his illegal activities secret if he admitted Jews or resistance workers to his clinic. The knowledge of his availability was passed by word of mouth, So Jews in need could find help, but eventually the wrong person was told, and the doctor was sent to a concentration camp, where he died. The books of Adler, Jung and Freud had been banned from our classes, but a few copies had survived the book burnings, and we shared these at our get-togethers, which was doubly dangerous. Not only would we have been arrested for possessing such books, but also if you expressed an opinion in class that came from one of those books, you would have been suspect at once. It was so difficult, always watching my tongue, never saying anything spontaneously for fear it would be misconstrued, or heard by the wrong person. It wasn't long before I became deeply involved in the underground. It was the only bright spot in a dreary, depressing world of lunatic politics.

It sounds exciting and thrilling, the word "underground", but my part was not much of a cloak and dagger role. I helped Jews get from one place to another, they weren't supposed to ride the trains any more, and I passed out leaflets containing anti-Nazi material. At one point, we distributed letters from the Bishop of Muenster Diocese throughout Breslau, and then copied off a hundred or so to be sent all over Germany. They were to be read from the pulpit, but often the Nazis prevented this, so our surreptitious copying helped spread the Bishop's encouragement. About a dozen of us took 10-12 letters each and went to different post offices in the area so that no one would be tipped off by a large bunch of similar-looking letters.

The people were so blind to the absurdity of banning or destroying all things "not German". They were unseeing disciples of the master race philosophy that told them they were superior to all nationalities. The most brilliant psychology experts were discounted because they were Jewish. The music of Mendelssohn could not be played, and Germany's nationally loved "Lorelei" could not be sung, because both the poet Heine and the great composer were Jews. Everywhere there were signs of Nicht Juden—No Jews—in the restaurants, stores, even on the benches in the park and on the buses and streetcars. All Jews had to wear a yellow star, or be sent to a concentration camp. During the first few years, not all Jews were forced into the camps. As late as 1936, Jews could still leave the country, if they could afford it financially. Businessmen were forced to sell out at a great loss, but if they wanted out, there was, at least, still a way. It is amazing how many of them didn't leave, because they didn't believe they were in any danger.

Some of them had fought in the World War, had even been decorated for bravery, and they laughed to think that this same country they had defended so honorably could kick them out or have them killed. They were either too trusting or too fatalistic, accepting the persecution as the will of God, and refusing to run from it.

Between the world wars, before Hitler took over, the Jewish people had more money, as a whole, than anybody else. They were good businessmen and they worked hard for their profits, but still there was resentment. A Jewish man in Breslau, Julius Kaufman, helped the people across the street when they went bankrupt. He dressed them from top to toe, and every day they ate at his house. Julius was a bachelor with no dependents, so he lavished his affection and wealth on this Gentile family. When Hitler came along with his Nazi Party and anti-Semitic glorification, they were some of the first to join, and sadly enough they saw to it that Julius was carried off to a camp. There were many good Jews like this Julius, but Hitler and his Nazis chose only to see the bad. Jewish generosity or sympathy only added fuel to a flame of resentful bigotry.

We could never see out of our cells in Nürnberg. The single window in the room was located at the very top of the wall and all the furniture was anchored to the floor, so you couldn't scoot something over to help reach the window. But in August, just before my trial, I was allowed to work in the kitchen, peeling potatoes, cleaning vegetables and washing the big kettles. This gave me a change of scenery, a chance to talk to the other workers, and a little bit more food, since we were allowed to eat the leftovers in the bottom of the kettles.

One of the women I met there had a big round face and crossed eyes that were small and dark brown like raisins. She had been a conductor on a train hauling soldiers back into Germany. One day as they passed a billboard, a soldier read aloud: "Räder müssen rollen für den Sieg" or "Wheels must roll for the victory". The conductress laughed sourly and said, "Huh! You'll be surprised when you come to Germany how the heads are rolling there." For that comment, she was sent to prison. We asked her time and again to tell the story, laughing harder each time as she squinted her tiny crossed eyes and complained indignantly, "And that dirty rat, he tattled on me. And here I am, six months, just for making a joke!" Another woman had written and sung a parody to a patriotic song about northern Germany. Instead of singing, "Where the waves are rolling in, there is my home", she said, "Where those wooden heads sit behind a door..." When we were alone, with no guard around, we sang her silly little song at the tops of our voices.

A transport train took about 50 of us to Munich in November. We were packed into a single car so tightly there was hardly room to stand. Four nights were spent sleeping on a cement floor, and then a second train headed us north toward Rothenfeld, a women's correction institute.

When I first saw the prison, I thought it was the most beautiful place I had ever seen. Clean, untracked snow lay around it like a white velvet mantle enfolding a turreted fortress: it had been a monastery or convent, and sat on a hill away from the forest. My lungs swelled as I sucked in the crisp winter air. I stopped for a moment, incredulous of this overabundance of elegant nature after tedious months of dull prison walls.

A rifle butt thrust into the small of my back sent me sprawling headfirst into the Rothenfeld velvet. "Clumsy swine," snarled the guard who had struck me. "Get up or I'll have to shoot you, and wouldn't that be too bad?"

My hands and feet dug into the snow as I scooted out of his reach like a scrawny displaced lobster.

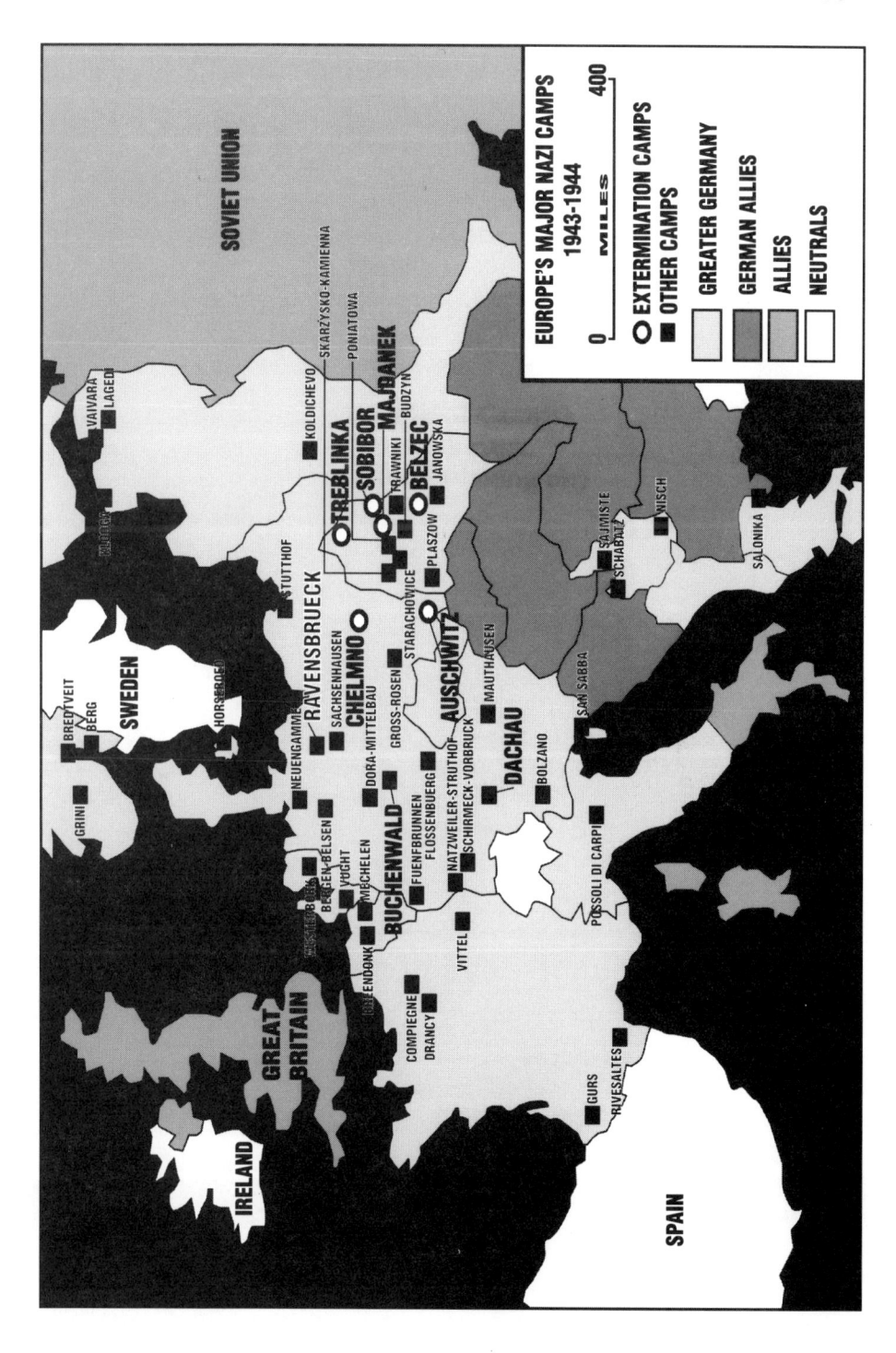

Condemned to Rothenfeld Prison 39

CHAPTER FOUR

Rothenfeld Prisoner #696

No drinking water—except what we got from melting snow in a bucket. The prison had no running water, and an oxen-drawn tank was used to haul water to the kitchen from a nearby lake. Two prisoners spent all day, under guard, filling and emptying the big barrel. Bitter "ersatz" coffee served in the morning before work was our only drink, but the food was mostly a kind of soup, so it was a good source of liquid.

My first job at Rothenfeld, after I was assigned the number 696, was to help knit socks for the soldiers. About 120 women worked in one knitting room and we weren't supposed to talk, but that was an altogether impossibility, although we were careful to converse in low tones. It was much like the monotonous murmuring sound of bees at work in a hive. The guard who sat with us each day became so accustomed to shouting "Ruhig sein!" at the slightest bit of real noise that one day when the whistle blew for lunch, she started, yelled, "Ruhig sein!", then blushed, and stammered, "Er, I mean, go out now."

In no time at all the overcrowded workroom, its various cliques, and the never-changing handiwork began to wear on my nerves, and I requested an interview with the warden, who was a woman this time. In fact, all of the prison guards were women, and the maintenance work was performed by the women prisoners. There was only one man and he served as an overseer of the work done on the estate that surrounded the prison. I asked to be transferred to the crew in the forest, bringing the warden's attention to my large stature and exaggerating how strong I was. I wanted to get out in the fresh air and get some exercise, but I also knew that forestry workers got more to eat, because of the heavy labor.

The initial work of sawing and cutting the trees by hand, trimming the branches and stripping off the bark brought the sweat popping out on our brows, even though it was mid-winter, and our muscles ached the first week from all the swinging and pulling we were unaccustomed to. But that work was relatively easy, compared to dragging the downed trees from where they had fallen on the road, to where they could be loaded on a truck. The women would pull one tree, leaning into a chain that went across their chests and then fastened onto the tree. We often fell because of the snow and mud, and if we didn't go fast enough to please the guards, we were whipped. I was glad to be out of the knitting room, but day by day my depression deepened and I wondered at night if I would pull through the few hours of sleep, and often I hoped that I wouldn't. I was lonely and bitter and desolate. I was sure that my family was dead or dying. I had nothing to live for, nothing to look forward to but endless days of strength-sapping labor and both physical and mental cruelty.

We gathered firewood and built a big fire when we first came to the woods in the morning, and every hour or so we were allowed to go back to it and warm our hands. Not that they felt sorry for us, it was necessary to enable us to continue working in the freezing temperatures. One day as I came back to the fire, I felt something in my shoe and started to sit on a stump to see what the problem was. I reached down and brushed the snow from the top of the dead tree trunk, revealing a bright green leaf that clung to the wood for life, even as it strained upward with a knowledge that it had to reach the sun and air because its parent had only so much left to give.

I had been in such a state of depression all day that the sight seemed to be an omen, something magic, a message. Just as here there is new life fighting to survive under the ice and snow, so will there be a new life for me when I come out of this darkness, if only I have faith, I told myself. The brave little dab of greenery had given me the strength and courage to go on. I prayed then as I hadn't for a long time, asking God to forgive me for my weakness and thanking Him for the message, asking him to help me remember that I was not alone, after all, and that I had much to live for and to give thanks for. My mother and my son would be waiting for me, expecting me to come home. I had to go on.

I remember...

I had gone to southern Switzerland to write my dissertation after leaving the University at Breslau, and it was there that I met Frans, my future husband. In February 1939, I moved into a little house in Ascona, at the Laga Maggiore, very near the Italian border. The man who owned the house wanted his children tutored in Dutch, because their mother had been Dutch, and I taught them in exchange for the rent. In the evenings, I could walk from my home on the Monte Veritá—Truth Mountain—down to the village and visit with the young people who gathered there. One evening in May, a group of us were at a dance in the tavern, discussing everything between heaven and earth, including politics, which we knew very little about. The music started up and a man sitting alone at the next table came over and asked me to dance. We talked about music and the people at the dance, and he brought me back to my table when the song ended. When another tune began, he came to me again and as we danced he explained that he was there on vacation. I asked him what he had seen so far, and advised him on other interesting places. The third time he asked me to dance, one of the fellows at my table said, "Wait a moment. This is the third time, after all." But I laughed and told him, "He's a good dancer. I don't object."

As we moved to the music, I asked, "Which part of Germany are you from?"

"From Germany?" my newly found friend asked. "I'm not from Germany, I'm from Holland."

I stopped dancing and stood in the middle of the floor, laughing hard. He looked at me with surprise and curiosity.

"Here we've both been talking our best school German and we are both from Holland. Yes, I'm from Holland, too," I explained.

"Well, I should have introduced myself," he said, and mentioned a surname that was very well known in Holland. He belonged to one of the oldest Dutch noble families.

Frans joined us at our table, and we danced and talked for the rest of the evening. He took me home in his car, a little two-seater, and asked if he could pick me up the next day, so we made a date for about four o'clock, when I would be finished working on my dissertation for the day. We drove to a little town just over the border into Italy and had dinner at a tiny cafe. The tables were in a small garden, and we were the only customers. Every day, he came and picked me up at four, and it didn't take long for me to fall in love with him. It wasn't on the first day, but soon after that, and I knew that he loved me too, but he didn't say so. In June, he had to go home to Holland, and we promised to write each other—one week I would write, the next week was his turn—and this went on until August.

In August 1939, the political situation was so dangerous that everyone who was not a Swiss national left the country. I packed my trunk and suitcase and took the train back to Holland. I reached home on August 28, after spending the night sitting on my suitcase in the train corridor, the cars were so crowded. The next day, Holland was declared in a state of war. Troops were mobilized, and in my hometown several schools were evacuated and the soldiers moved in. On an errand to the post office on August 30, I turned from the window to see Frans, resplendent in an air force captain's uniform. What a surprise! He thought I was still in Ascona, and I had no idea he had been assigned to the airfield outside my hometown. We were so happy that we chattered like school children as we walked toward my home. Frans maneuvered my bicycle to one side so that I could walk next to him.

As we approached my house, we met my mother, who was on her way to town to do some shopping. When she saw me with this soldier, she froze, then greeted me coolly. After she passed us, I said, "Frans, that was my mother."

"Well, I would like to meet your mother," he said. "Is it alright if I come tonight at about seven o'clock?" I told him that would be fine, and we said goodbye.

Mother was furious when she returned. "Yesterday, the soldiers came to town. Today, I see my youngest daughter running around with one of them. Haven't you any feeling of decency?" I tried to explain that Frans was a friend whom I had met in Switzerland, but she said that had nothing to do with it. "Girls who run after soldiers are the worst kind," she said disapprovingly. To her, it made no difference that he was an officer; everybody was a soldier to her, from corporal to general. When I mumbled that he had asked to be introduced to her that evening, she sniffed and said, "At least he has some manners." She was always very much for manners and what people would think or say.

The moment I introduced Frans to my mother, he asked me to leave them alone so he could speak to her in private. My mother said, "You can go to your room." They were treating me as if I were a child! I was slightly miffed and very curious as I sat in my room, waiting for them to call me back, and wondering what Frans was up to.

About ten minutes later, Mother called me down to the parlor and announced, "I'm happy to be the first to congratulate you on your engagement."

"What engagement?" I cried and she beamed. Frans had realized immediately what kind of person my mother was, and he had asked her permission to marry me before he had even broached the subject to his prospective bride. But I had no objections.

We got engaged officially at Christmas. In Holland, an engagement is almost like a wedding. Printed announcements are sent out, gifts are received, and a big dinner with flowers and all the trimmings is held for friends and relatives.

Soon after he had met Mother, Frans told me, "Now you have to go with me to The Hague." That was where his father lived. "But I have to warn you. My father is very old-fashioned and strict. You'd better not put on any make-up and don't go to the hairdresser. The best thing would be to wear your hair in a bun. Dress very conservatively."

Frans had no brothers or sisters—he was an only child—and his mother was dead. There was only his father to contend with, but I thought, "Oh, brother, how will I ever please a man like that?" We came to The Hague and Frans let us in the front entrance with a key he had. At the end of a long, marble corridor, another door opened just as we began to walk down the hall. A well-dressed, white-haired man came out and looked at us for a moment with a serious, appraising expression. Then he broke into a grin, opened his arms, and cried, "I have always wanted a daughter, my dear, and now I have one."

Frans had fooled me. His father was not at all severe or strict. All the way to The Hague I had been almost shivering with apprehension. This was where the diplomatic corps and people of the ministries were, and they were regarded as snobs. A familiar joke at that time was that the people in The Hague carried their potatoes home from the market in a violin case, because even though they were human enough to need to eat, they couldn't bear to be seen doing anything so mundane as carrying a shopping bag home.

But his father was a wonderful man, and to me it was like suddenly gaining a father for myself, after all those years of never having known my own. When the war started, Frans' father had to go to England with the government because he was one of the queen's unofficial advisors. He died there during the war—not during a raid, but of natural causes—and I don't know if he ever knew what had happened to his son.

It seems now that Frans and I spent so much of our time together laughing and thoroughly enjoying each other and the world around us. One Saturday in April 1940, we went to the beach. It was early in the season, and it hadn't been cleaned for the tourists yet, and as we ran down the edge of the water, we jumped and stumbled over all kinds of driftwood and debris, even a seal carcass. We spent nearly two hours wandering across the sand in the crisp sea air, holding hands and talking, teasing each other and trying to trip one another. We studied the twisted, salt encrusted wood and fantasized about where each piece had come from, and how it had survived its ocean cruise. Finally, we froze out and went up the steps from the beach to a cozy, dark restaurant, where we drank coffee and ate little pastries, licking the crumbs and sticky topping off our fingers. There was a dog wandering around through the tables, and as he neared our table, I was trying to cut my pastry with a fork, but my fingers were stiff from the cold. The bun flew off my saucer and onto the floor in front of the dog. He gobbled it up. Frans said I was clumsy, but I blamed it on the dog, reasoning that he couldn't defend himself, no matter what I accused him of. Frans just laughed, shook his head, muttered something about female logic and kissed my hand. We looked at each other and grinned, laughing together at nothing in particular the way people in love often do.

Nothing could lift me higher or make me feel more important than the thought that Frans loved me. We spent as much time together as we possibly could, and even when he was on duty and working hard to put his squadron through the proper air exercises. Sometimes a "V" of five planes would dip over the roof of our house, and I knew that then, too, my love was thinking of me.

Back to Prison...

The Rothenfeld warden and overseer soon realized that it was not satisfactory employing women in the woods. French prisoners of war were brought in with oxen, and of course, since I was suspected of helping just such Kriegsgefangener, I was removed from the woods at once. I went to work in the fields. It was hard work, sometimes harder than skidding trees by hand had been, but the agricultural crew got only the same small amount of food that the knitters got.

The guard, Fraulein Hermann, had something against me from the very start, too. Other women worked in pairs or trios, packing in the sacked potatoes, but I had to work alone, carrying each bag myself, balancing the heavy, awkward load on my shoulder as I stumbled over the plowed ground. One day we planted potatoes and the guard came up behind me and said, "Don't you see there is one uncovered?" I couldn't see a potato anywhere. "If you can't see it with your eyes, six-ninety-six, I'll put your nose on it so you can sniff it out." She took me by the neck and forced me down until my face was in the dirt. Something sharp dug into my neck on both sides—I don't know if it was her nails or something sharp she held in her hands—but there was nothing I could do to stop her. Another time, I was trying to fix a conveyor belt that had slipped and Fraulein Hermann reached over and turned the machine on without warning. I could have lost both my hands.

The part I hated most about agriculture was clearing the rocks from the fields. Two women would share a wire basket between them, filling it with rocks as they made their way down the length of the field. All day long, we stayed bent over. Any time we tried to straighten and stretch our backs, there was a guard with a whip to bend us back over. On the way home in the evening, after all day without water, we stayed half bent over, our skin sunburned, every bone aching, our tongues swollen with thirst.

There was only one other woman in my prison dormitory who was not a criminal, although she was classified as such, and that was 68-year-old Julie Geuther, condemned to six months in prison for giving a Jew a piece of bread. Little Julie could never sleep at night because her feet got so cold, so I would take her skirt, hold it against the tiles of the fireplace until the material was hot, then run over to her bed and wrap the skirt around her feet. Her big brown eyes always reflected such gratitude. She told me that her 80-year-old husband was home alone, because none of their children had been told about their mother's imprisonment. It was a terrible scandal, and their jobs—many of them high positions, would have been imperiled by knowledge of their mother's traitorous deed. The old man died there by himself when his wife had been in prison for about three months. Julie's sentence was then cut in half, and she was allowed to leave. She just shook her head mournfully at me the day she went home. We were given no chance to say goodbye.

Reality was so awful that I began fantasizing about many different things in search of an escape from the sordidness of prison life. It was in Rothenfeld that I first began building my dream house.

It was so beautiful...

Wild magenta roses climb over the white arched latticework of the garden gate and a gray flagstone path, bordered by bright orange poppies, tall stately dahlias and clean white daisies leads past a round brick water well to the kitchen door. The top half of the wooden door is open, and morning sunlight reflects off the polished red tile on the kitchen floor. Copper kettles and utensils shine above the wood stove. My freshly harvested light yellow wheat lies in a clean burlap bag, waiting to be ground and then mixed and baked into bread, and potatoes and vegetables from my garden simmer in a soup on the stove. One door leads to my bedroom—austere, with only a bed, a simple oak dresser and a ladder-backed chair. Another door opens into the living room, its floor covered with oriental rugs. The big overstuffed couch and chairs go well with the lace-covered dining room table that fits so snugly into this end of the room, its attendant chairs placed at precise intervals along its roundness. In the ceiling is the little door that opens to let a light staircase down for access to the attic bedroom where my nieces and nephews sometimes stay.

Outside, a golden brown milk cow and hairy pink pig lie warm and contented on the sunny side of the barn. Chickens feed along the green banks of the creek, clucking to themselves and sometimes calling out to one another. My rabbits are hidden in the berry bushes, perhaps thinking about making nuisances of themselves in my big vegetable garden. I live not too far from town, but just on the edge of the woods, so I can slip into the shaded quiet of the forest and pick blueberries, eating them with a lump and a dab of the good sweet cream I separate from the cow's milk each time I milk her, sometimes I let her fat half-grown baby have it all.

Somehow, I never, in all those years, got around to designing a bathroom. And I never imagined the curtains or shades at my windows. The language the women in Rothenfeld used was unbelievably filthy. One night that I dared object to their talk, about a dozen of them rushed over, tore off my blanket and gown, and started pinching me all over. I was horrified and sick to my stomach. But another night, it got so bad that I threatened to tell the warden and ask for a transfer to another dormitory. The next morning, I was called into the warden's office and told that she had received numerous complaints about the vile words I had been using at night. When I protested my innocence, the warden sighed and said she could hardly take my word alone above half a dozen other prisoners' statements. Not only were they despicable liars, but also the women stole anything they could get their hands on. Once a week, for example, each of us was issued a patty of margarine on a small square of cardboard. As I was walking back to my bed one day, someone called my name. I turned to answer and felt a movement at my hand. When I looked back at the little cardboard in my palm, the margarine was gone, and none of the women around me would look me in the eye.

It was December 1941. The Germans entered Moscow on the fourth, while back home the Winterhilfe appeal had their families scrounging for warm clothing for the troops. Pearl Harbor, Hawaii, was attacked by the Japanese three days later and America plunged head first into the war so many of her people had tried to ignore. Roosevelt made a war speech against Japan on December 8 and in another three days Germany declared war on the United States.

I dreamt of growing up...

The heavy scent of roasting geese, seasoned and basted and watched over carefully, filled the late afternoon air, accompanied by the thrilling sweetness of pudding and cake smells. It was Christmas Eve, and everyone on Grossvater's estate waited impatiently for the ceremony and the reward of the annual servants' dinner. All the people who worked for Grossvater, as well as their families, were invited to dinner in the castle every Christmas Eve. Their august employer, his son and—as soon as I was old enough—his granddaughter, would serve these hard working people in recognition of and thanks for their efforts with the crops, animals and the running of the house. Everyone there got a Christmas gift—no big things, just little useful items—starting with the oldest member of the staff. No one was ever fired by Grossvater because of old age. They were given a pension when they became unable to work, and lived out the rest of their lives in one of Grossvater's cottages, near their life-long friends and in the company of their family. Because of the custom of beginning the gift-giving with the oldest and then working down chronologically, I was almost the last one to receive my gift. It was hard for me to wait, I was never a patient child, and I would be fidgeting and straining to see what was in the packages, and how close it was to my turn.

We always had a tall, tall Christmas tree in the dining room, its pointed top stretching to touch the near-darkness at the high ceiling. I wasn't allowed to see the tree until the heavy double doors were opened at night for the servants' dinner. Then the special warm "green" smell would tickle our noses as everyone sucked in their breath and then released an appreciative "ahh". The long, linen-covered table was decorated with sharp-pointed leaves of holly with tiny, bright red berries, and tall white candles that gave off warm, wavering light. I especially anticipated the moment when the weihnachtstollen, a raisin-filled cake dusted with powdered sugar, was served.

After dinner, we bundled up for a ride to the village church, 45 minutes away by horse and buggy. Blankets and furs were piled on top of Grossvater and me, and snuggled down around me until I could barely see out, and I certainly couldn't move. I could watch the tiny stars in the black sky pass out of sight over my head, hear the sharp rhythmic beating of the horses' hooves against the frozen ground, feel the warmth on one side of me that was Grossvater. It happened once that it had snowed the day before Christmas, and we rode to church in a horse-drawn sleigh, bells jingling and my happiness soaring. It never failed that I was too excited to take my required afternoon nap on such a day. I had to spend the time in my bed, but the anticipation of the approaching dinner, gift-giving and moonlit ride was just too much for one little mind to calmly contemplate. So in the evening, full of goose and cake, sparked by the chill night air, and then lulled by the warmth of the church and the dull words of a sermon aimed at adults, I would succumb to sleep, my head tipping and my body relaxing until I fit quite naturally into the side of Grossvater's bulk.

Back in Holland, the emphasis was on Christmas Day, rather than the night before, and the observance began at 4:30 in the morning with a mass. Before we went to bed on Christmas Eve, we got our holiday clothing out of the closet in the front room where it was kept, because the tree would be decorated after we went to bed, and we couldn't see it until we came back from church. Mother had a special low table for the crèche— the Nativity scene. The table was brought down from the fourth floor only at Christmas time, placed before the tree, and covered with a white sheet. We children would go into the forest and gather moss, putting it on the table and then setting up the big stable and figurines on the natural yellow-green base, with a background painted to depict the houses and streets of Bethlehem. The Three Wise Men were not included in the Nativity scene until January 6—Epiphany.

After church, we always had a very festive breakfast. One of the pastors who served in our church always came home with us to share this holiday meal. "Nowhere do they celebrate Christmas the way this family does," he would say to Mother. My sister would play the piano, one brother the violin, another brother the flute, and the rest of us would fill the holy day with the words of old German Christmas songs.

It was my first Christmas in prison, and everyone in Rothenfeld was excited about the coming holiday, even though we were locked up in a dirty, drafty jail far from our families and friends. Wherever women were gathered for more than a few minutes, the question always came up: "What do you think they'll give us as a Christmas treat?" Many of the women had spent more than one Christmas behind bars, and they reminisced about what they had been given by prison authorities as their only Christmas gifts. In Stuttgart, it had been sausage; in another, an apple and orange; cookies at a third.

The afternoon of December 24, we assembled in the chapel for Christmas prayers and songs, led by a Catholic priest, Presbyterian minister and the Rothenfeld warden. At six o'clock, we had our regular dull meal, then went to our unlit rooms where we again told the stories of earlier Christmases. We poked each other in the ribs, joking about who would be the first to cry with homesickness, then made each other promise there would be no tears or sadness. After all, it was a time of celebration, and soon we would have our little treat of special food, and this time next year, we'd be looking back on this day from the shelter of our homes. "Come now, girls, let's have some wagers on what we're going to be eating, soon as they bring it 'round."

Outside, the first wheezy accordion notes began and crept into the sound of our jovial conversation. There was an immediate silence as the first words of "Silent Night" came from the throats of our prison guards. Then we realized, as we lay or sat in our darkened realm of captivity, that our only treat was a heartfelt song.

From every bed came the sound of anguished sobs.

CHAPTER FIVE

From Prison to Concentration Camp for Life

At Rothenfeld, prisoners were allowed mail from home and when I got the first letter from Mother, I sat and held it for a long time, seeing in my mind's eye her long, slender fingers and pale vein-lined hands holding the pen that had made the strokes on the paper I gripped. She was well. Baby Frans was growing and healthy. My heart soared. I wrote back on a tiny scrap of paper, telling her that my time was almost up and that I could receive a package from home, if she had anything to send. I was to be released May 8, 1942.

But two weeks prior to my projected day of freedom, I made a terrible mistake. We were working outside the prison, gathering and chopping firewood, guarded by Fraulein Hermann, the one who hated me so much. We were talking among ourselves about how much time we had left and I smiled and said, "I have only two weeks to go."

"I wouldn't be so cocksure, if I were you," Hermann sneered. "Have you never heard about 'concentration camp'?" The thought had never occurred to me. My time was up; I would be leaving this hole. I would leave and not look back, if I had to walk the whole way, I was on my way to see my baby.

"Do you mean I will have to go to a camp?" My voice quivered with sudden fright and dread. It was like someone had thrown cold water in my face.

"I didn't say that," Hermann smiled. "I just wouldn't be so sure of myself, if I were you."

"I have to go and ask the warden about this," I said hesitantly.

"You're not going anywhere," Hermann warned me.

"Oh, yes," I insisted, my thoughts reeling. "I have to know. I have to get this cleared up. I have to." I put down my axe and ran back to the prison, out of breath as I pounded on the warden's office door, only to find that she wasn't there. I leaned against the wall, gulping in air as my heart raced from the exertion and worry. Now what? Now what? Now what? is all my brain could register as I pushed away from the wall and ran back to my work unit. But it was too late. Hermann had already reported that I had thrown away my work tool, refused to work and left the work site without permission. It was the same as trying to escape.

I was called into the warden's office the next day, and she told me I had been sentenced to four weeks extra after my regular time was up, under "severe arrest". On May 7, the day before I would have been going home, they showed me my food package from home. There was a whole loaf of bread, a pound cake, a little honey cake, a tin box stuffed with oatmeal cookies, yellow cheese, sticky artificial honey, five white hard boiled eggs and a mug of rich golden butter.

"What do you want done with this?" one guard asked. "Save it for you or let the people in sick bay have it?"

"I want it for when I come out!" I shouted, my stomach growling and churning at the anticipation of real homemade, pleasure giving, taste bud-pleasing, fresh food. "My mother sent that for me. I have been looking forward to it for a long time."

They put me in a cell in the basement. There was no table, no chair. A low wooden platform attached to the wall would serve as my bed, and there was a bucket—with a lid on it, this time—in the corner. This was on a Friday, and I didn't get anything to eat until Tuesday. That day, they brought me water and bread. My next meal was four days later, and after that, every third day. Two days with nothing at all, one day with water and bread. And on the day I was fed, they brought me a blanket to cover myself with at night. Nights can be quite cold in Germany in May. But the woman who was in charge there, Fraulein Brantmayer, a very nice woman, had given me the cell next to the kitchen, so one wall was always warm from the cooking heat. I didn't suffer too much from the cold. But from hunger. Oh, the never-ending pain of hunger.

I had been hungry before, working hard with little to eat, and suffering through the hours of night until the morning came with its cup of ersatz coffee and stale crust of bread. But now it had become hard to even tell morning from night. The first couple of days, there was only the familiar ache in my stomach. The third day, it was like my stomach had forgotten it was empty because there was no pain; I was just thirsty and listless. But then my head began to ache and every time I moved from my shelf-bed, there were bright dots in front of my eyes—the only "light" I had. So I stopped moving from my shelf, and spent hour after hour just lying in one position, not even thinking. During the first week or so, I found myself straining to hear some sound, perhaps a kettle dropped in the kitchen, or someone passing through the corridor, but it didn't take long before I gave that up. There were no sounds. Only my breathing and my heartbeat, and sometimes I didn't hear them.

A guard came with a prisoner to empty the waste bucket in my cell some mornings—after a few days of nothing to eat or drink, there wasn't much need for the bucket—but it was not always the same guard. One day, a young guard came, I think her name was Fraulein Meyering, and did something that could have landed her in prison herself. After the prisoner had put the emptied bucket down and started to leave the cell, the guard strode after her, hesitating only long enough to fling a piece of bread back towards me. If anyone had known that, she would have been imprisoned and harshly punished.

After three weeks, the woman in charge—Brantmayer—could see that I wasn't going to make it another week. She called in the guard who took care of the sick prisoners, a rough type, but she was just and had a good heart. She checked my pulse, looked in my eyes and at my tongue. Maybe ten minutes later, the lieutenant warden came to my cell, a beautiful woman with big brown eyes and wavy hair who had the deep, commanding voice of a sergeant major. She looked at me and frowned, saying, "Six-nine-six, I was here last week and wanted to do something for you, but when I asked you how you felt, you said, 'Fine, I've never felt better'."

I closed my eyes for a moment. My hair was stiff and greasy, my body stank. I was so weak that at night when I heard mice scampering across the stone floor and up the legs of my shelf, I only lay there, letting them run across me, not caring enough to move a hand. I had a son at home who needed his mother. I had a mother, too, who prayed daily for my return.

"Yes, I know what I said," I finally croaked. "But I am at the end of my rope. I am ready to admit that I can't make it."

Brantmayer strode out of the cell, and within minutes guards came in, bringing me a clean dress and apron, a shawl and some water to wash myself. They took me to the warden, and she said, "Johanna, I hope that you have learned by now that you cannot use your head to butt your way through a brick wall." I was so weak and exhausted, hungry and aching, so glad to be let out of my lonely, dark cell; I just stood there without saying anything. I hadn't the strength to argue the fine points of who had been right or wrong.

The guards put me in a cell by myself, the departure cell, where prisoners were put just prior to going home. They brought me my mother's food package, and I lifted the box, remembering the treats that awaited me. The loaf of bread was green with mold. I had to throw it out. I cut half the pound cake away. The butter was rancid, the eggs were spoiled. I salvaged the cheese, because they say it has to be moldy to be good, so I only trimmed its fur coat. I hadn't cried in all those weeks of isolated misery in the basement, but I cried then. Here Mother had put that together for me, when they had so little to eat in Holland during the war, saving it from her few rations, depriving herself, and it had to spoil. I cried then, like a little child.

I got lots and lots to eat in that cell, from Saturday to Monday. I had books to read, a comfortable bed. On Monday, I prepared to go to Munich. Shortly before I was to leave, Brantmayer, the guard from the basement, came to me. Even this was a risk, because guards weren't allowed to do things on their own. She took my hands in hers, and the tears streamed down her face as she said, "Six-nine-six, Johanna, whatever happens to you, whatever awaits you, don't forget that you have a mother at home who expects to see you again." Then she ran from the cell.

I was confused by what she had told me, and the obvious grief that she felt for me. What could it mean? But before I could give it much thought, a guard came to get me and I was outside the walls of Rothenfeld—free at last! I had a smile on my face that would not go away. They brought me to the main road, where we waited for the bus. A man who came on the bus took my papers and me to Munich. I waited four days until a group was assembled, and then we went by train to Nürnberg. All of us were put in a big room, not in the same prison I had started out in, for it had been

Unleserliche und schlecht lesbare Briefe können nicht zensiert werden und werden vernichtet

**Frauen - Konzentrationslager
Ravensbrück
Fürstenberg i. Meckl.**

Auszug aus der Lagerordnung:

Jede Schutzhaftgefangene darf im Monat einen Brief oder eine Karte absenden oder empfangen. Die Zeilen müssen mit Tinte, übersichtlich und gut lesbar geschrieben sein. Briefe dürfen vier normale Seiten mit je 15 Zeilen und Karten 10 Zeilen nicht überschreiten. Jedem Schreiben darf nur eine 12 Rpf. Briefmarke beigefügt werden, weitere verfallen der Beschlagnahme zugunsten mittelloser Häftlinge. Fotos dürfen nicht geschickt werden. Alle Postsendungen müssen mit Häftlings- oder Blocknummer versehen sein. Pakete jeglichen Inhalts dürfen nicht empfangen werden. Es kann im Lager alles gekauft werden. Geldsendungen sind zulässig, müssen aber durch Postanweisung erfolgen. Nationalsozialistische Zeitungen sind zulässig, müssen aber vom Häftling selbst über die Postzensurstelle des Frauen-Konzentrationslagers bestellt werden. Entlassungsgesuche aus der Schutzhaft an die Lagerleitung sind zwecklos.

Der Lagerkommandant

Meine genaue Anschrift:

Johanna Krön

Nr. 22442

Block Z

Fr.-Konz.-Lager Ravensbrück
Fürstenberg i. Meckl.

Ravensbrück, den November 43.

First page of a letter written by Johanna to her mother, Nov. 1943.

bombed, and we waited for 11 days. What could be holding us up? I asked myself daily. But my thoughts were filled more with my homecoming and seeing my son. I tried to conjure up a mental picture of this small being who was a part of me and of Frans, the dearest person in my life. What did baby Frans look like? Mother hadn't even told me the color of his hair. Did he have brown eyes like his father, or blue like mine? Surely he would be walking by now, and perhaps talking. I wonder if he says "Mama"? With mischievous Frans and me for parents, I bet he has trouble with his grandmother. She will think she is being punished by having another Johanna to raise.

My thoughts turned to Mother. When I read her letters, I could see her hands, but her face was a blur. I had a kind of amnesia after I came out of the Nürnberg torture chamber, perhaps caused by the constant shaking of my head for so many days. I could remember the flat wedding band Mother wore, picture it on her long, slender fingers, but the lines and contours of her face escaped me. I had memorized the lines of every letter and post card. We were allowed to receive one letter a month and to write home once monthly. Why was it that I could not bring back her face?

I prayed then that my mother had been able to keep herself and baby Frans well. As my first-born, he was terribly precious to me, and my life had seemed to center upon his well-being, now that I was sure I would never have another child. I had experienced a normal amount of discharge following his birth, but since then, for a year, I had not had a monthly flow. I suppose it was a combination of the tortures they submitted me to, and the starvation and hard work, but whatever the cause, I never menstruated again.

I knew the psychological effects such treatment could have, from my studies in psychology at Breslau. It had taken me a year of faithful attendance at the university in Amsterdam, studying foreign languages, before my mother could be convinced to allow me to pursue my interest in medicine. She saw it, I guess, as a public service, a means of making sure I provided for the care of others, rather than only for myself. I'm sure the analyses of Jung and Freud, theories we studied by candlelight for fear of discovery, helped me cope with the trauma I encountered daily.

A guard took me out of the room where I was staying and up to the second floor of the prison. I was told to sign some papers and began to read the contents.

"You don't have to read them," the guard snapped. "Just sign them, and let's get this over with."

"I cannot sign without knowing what it is I am putting my name to," I started to argue. How could I have forgotten I was in Nazi Germany, and arguments were not allowed? He struck me and kicked me, shouting that I must sign. I was bewildered at this treatment; the blows and kicks were too much. Just let me go home, please.

They gave me a copy of the papers after I signed the last page, and I was hurried back to the communal cell. As I began to read the document, I suddenly became dizzy and leaned against the wall, sliding down until I was sitting on the floor, my knees bent almost until they touched my face, the unbelievable papers lying on my thighs, the words fat and gloating on the page. My eyes blurred with tears and I struggled to focus on the typed sentences. It was Schutzhaft, the words told me. I was a danger to the German people because of my crimes against their nation, my falsification of documents. For my own protection I was to be transported and admitted to a Konzentrationslager—for life.

> Halte Schritt Kamerad und verlier nicht den Mut
> Keep in step, comrade, and lose not courage
>
> Denn wir haben den willen zurn Leben im Blut
> For we have the will to live in our blood
>
> Und im Herzen, im Herzen den Glauben.
> And in our hearts, in our hearts, the faith.
>
> O Ravensbrück, ich kann Dich nicht vergessen,
> Oh, Ravensbrück, I can't forget you,
>
> Weil Du mein Schicksal bist.
> Because you are my destiny.
>
> Wer Dich verlässt, der kann es erst ermessen
> Only she who leaves you can measure
>
> wie wundervoll die Freiheit ist.
> How wonderful freedom is.

O Ravensbrück, wir jarnrnern nacht und klagen,
Oh, Ravensbrück, we don't whine nor complain,

Was irnrner unsere Zukimft einrnal sei.
Whatever our future will be,

wir wollen "Ja" zurn Leben sagen,
We will say "Yes" to life,

Denn einrnal kornrnt der Tag, dann sind wir wieder frei.
Then the day will come that we are free again.

Johanna

CHAPTER SIX

Ravensbrück – Concentration Camp for #20442

Nearly 90 kilometers north of Berlin, Ravensbrück was built in 1935 for 10,000 female prisoners. I was number 20,442. It contained 35,000 women at the end of the war. I arrived with a group of about 50 other women in the evening of Thursday, June 17, 1942. We stood outside the camp and watched column after column of singing, uniformed workers file through the gates. It didn't take long to learn that the singing was mandatory—it kept the prisoners from talking and led outsiders to believe they were happy with their imprisonment. It took about an hour for the workers to get past and for guards to set up tables to check us in. A prisoner at a typewriter asked for our names and date of birth, and classified us as political, criminal or asocial prisoners. Then we were given a slip of cloth with our number stamped on it to be sewn on our uniform. In addition, I got a red triangle with an "N" painted on it, indicating I was a political prisoner from the Netherlands. Green meant criminal; black, asocial or gypsy; blue, no nationality; purple, Jehovah's witness; red with yellow bar, Jew or half-Jew; yellow triangle placed at an angle over a black triangle to form a star, woman who had had an intimate relationship with a Jew.

Jehovah's Witnesses were in the camp voluntarily. All they had to do was sign a paper saying they wouldn't preach any more—

they preached against Hitler—and they could go home. But they refused. They worked on farms outside the camp and left each morning without guards, because there was no question of them running away. They got enough to eat on the farms and came home in the evening with onions, potatoes and carrots. If you would listen to their preaching and follow their ways, you had it made—they fed you. Sometimes there was an absolute wave of salvation through the whole underfed camp.

The Jehovah's Witnesses said roll call was Hitler's idea, not the way of Jehovah, and they wouldn't come out for it. We had to stand in formation until everyone was there, and when these conscientious objectors wouldn't come, some of us had to go get them. I often got picked to roust them out because I was tall, and the guards figured I must also be strong. But the Jehovah's Witnesses were fat from eating outside the camp, while we were weak from lack of food, and they made themselves heavy and struggled against us. It usually took four or five of us to wrestle one of them. One day I got so mad that I dropped one of them in a puddle of rainwater, telling her, "You can sit there 'til you rot."

Once all the new prisoners had been classified and registered, we were herded into a bath hall. There was a long table with several people behind it, and we had to totally strip and parade by these people, as we were checked in every orifice for hidden jewelry or other valuables. Fifty unwashed, smelly, fish-belly-white bags of bones quailed before the impersonal, yet intruding, eyes of the guards, using our reddened, scaling hands in varying degrees of attempts at modesty, straining to keep from the ultimate intimacy of contact with warm, unknown skin. They shaved off my hair. It is quite a debasement for a woman to be robbed of such an adornment, to be masculinized and numbered—to be dehumanized. But they were looking for lice, and I had them, so off came the hair. A bored looking doctor then looked in our eyes and mouths, and down our throats, waving us on to the luxury of a warm shower—my last for another three years.

We were issued undershirt, pants, dress, wooden clogs and a little cotton towel. Our summer uniform was blue-gray with short sleeves. In the winter, we wore a dress of blue and off-white vertical stripes. Then we were assigned to Barracks 11, the "new arrival" unit—built for about 270 and holding nearly 450 women when I arrived.

Guards were very seldom in camp—prisoners were in charge of the barracks. A blockova was in charge of the barracks; two stubovas served under her, each one responsible for her own side. The barracks were divided into "Side A" and "Side B", with a washroom and toilets in between. Barracks 11 had a bank robber from Vienna as blockova. She habitually cut slices off everyone's bread ration and kept the extra for herself, but there was nothing we could do about it, since all complaints had to go through the blockova. There wasn't room in the barracks for everyone to sit down under those crowded conditions, so we took turns sitting and had to stand for long periods of time. We sat at the tables because it was against the rules to lie on your bed, but even that rule came to be ignored as the war dragged on.

So many Germans say now, "We were never Nazi." And I ask, "Were you not a member of the Party?" "Oh, yes, but we had to be." That is not true. Or they tell you, "But we didn't know that there were concentration camps."

I lived in Germany long before I was imprisoned there, and the abbreviation "KZ" for Konzentrationslager was used frequently, even in the 1930s. But as soon as it was mentioned, in whatever manner, someone would say, "Let's not talk about that. We don't want to know." They knew something terrible was going on in their own country, but they chose to ignore it. I worked in the Siemens factory outside Ravensbrück when I first came to the camp, and our supervisors were not SS men, but civil personnel. These upright, patriotic German family men saw each day the living skeletons who marched in under guard to work for them. How could the existence of the camps be known to no one?

They used to tell a story in Germany, and also in camp, about two Germans, Meyer and Muller, who met on the street. Meyer said to Muller, "Hey, I heard you were in the concentration camp. Is that true?" "Yes," said Muller, "that is true. I just came home last week." "Well, now, tell me, just in confidence between the two of us," Meyer said, "how was it there? You hear such strange stories." "It was fine," Muller insisted. "They woke us up about nine in the morning, even brought us breakfast in bed. When we had showered and were dressed, we went for walks and talked with each other, played cards or chess. We had lunch at about one—a good lunch—then in the afternoon we went to matinees. After dinner, we had a few drinks, then went to the movies. That was it." Meyer frowned. "That is strange. I heard about Schultz. He was in the camp, too, but he told a totally different story." Muller smiled sadly. "Yes, he told a different story, and that is why he is back there now again."

Don't think that all those years I was in captivity were never ending moments of agony. Had it been so, I wouldn't be here today. Our humor was often desperately contrived, but still, it kept the spirit up. We sang, danced, and told jokes, held discussions on everything from French literature to politics and religion. Sometimes we held "tea parties" like little girls, sharing the contents of a package sent from home. The work was hard and never-ending. Food was scarce, and what we got was tasteless, moldy, soggy or bone-dry hard. Everywhere there was filth, lice, and disease. But if I could, for even five minutes, laugh and forget the frightening prospect of the "here and now", then something was gained.

Some people ask, "How can there be a God when he put you through all those hardships?" I found out quite early that we don't always know why things happen. Sometimes we rebel, and afterwards, we see that it was all for the good. When I think back on the things I went through, I am grateful that I was in the concentration camp. I wouldn't be as mentally strong as I am today, I wouldn't be as happy as I am. I couldn't possibly appreciate things the way I do, if I hadn't had to sacrifice so much. Sometimes I thought, maybe this is to punish me for the wrong I have done. I was a wild kid, and when I grew up, I still had a strong sense of independence, a need to be free of restraint. That got me into trouble. The way I was brought up was to do things the way Mother wanted them done. Mother decided everything, and I never dared contradict her, except in my heart, which was many times. I showed that rebellion, too, in my face. The expression there always gave my thoughts away.

But I think that Christ took away all earthly love, all human love, from my life so that my heart would be empty and He could come and fill it with His love. I feel that love so clearly every day. When I drive in my car, I sing praises to the Lord for making such a beautiful world and allowing me to be part of it. I feel such gratitude when I awake in the morning and I thank Him that I have been brought through the night again. Then in the evening, I thank Him for all the things I have enjoyed during the day. I learned that God is behind all that. Things don't happen by themselves.

On Sundays there was only one roll call, held in the afternoon when we weren't working. But the first Sunday I was there, we were punished for something and forced to stand in formation for four hours under a summer sun. My shaved head burned badly. The next day, I was told my luggage had come—thanks to German preciseness, my belongings accurately followed me wherever I went—and I walked to the luggage room to check out the suitcase. When I got there, the room was unattended and locked, so I sat down exhausted on a luggage cart, falling asleep almost immediately. I hadn't been getting much rest at night because during the day another woman slept in my bed, and someone had told her that putting urine on her bald head would help the hair grow back faster. No matter which way I turned my head that smell seemed to reach me and force me to awake.

Coarse shouting pierced my slumber and I opened my bleary eyes to see the luggage room guard bent over me, angry at finding such a disheveled, stinking specimen at her door. She called me Schiessbudenfigur—shooting gallery figure—because of my bald head, and I confusedly asked, "Who me?"

"Do you think I mean myself, Drecksau?" She began hitting me over the head with her shoulder bag. I was too weak to fight back, even though the pain from her blows on my tender, scorched head were excruciating. At last, she stopped beating me and allowed me to sign for the luggage. As I walked back through camp, the hot tears flowed down my face. I was oblivious to the people around me. How much longer can I bear this, I wondered. It seems forever since I was arrested, and the end is nowhere in sight. Let's see, it was May 7, 1941 when the Gestapo arrested me, and today is...I stumbled, then stopped in disbelief. Today is June 21, 1942, Johanna. Today you are 27 years old.

After about a week, I was allowed to take tests for employment in the Siemens und Halske factory that had been set up, not far from the camp. It had been originally at Berlin-Charlottenbourg, just outside Berlin, but because of the obvious threat of bombing to the factory that made small parts for German aircraft and radios, the Nazis had moved the whole works to Ravensbrück. The English couldn't tell from the air which was the factory and which was a camp full of prisoners of war, so they wouldn't dare bomb the site. After my experience in Nürnberg prison, I hoped they were right.

It was a privilege to work in the Siemens factory, even though the work was hard, because we were sheltered from the weather, less likely to be beaten daily, and it was much better than being put on latrine detail or something worse. We unloaded heavy machinery from railroad cars, and I was still weak from the weight loss and inactivity of severe arrest at Rothenfeld. One day, I couldn't hold up my end of a machine any longer, and I dropped it, breaking something. Another prisoner told the guard I had done it on purpose, an act of sabotage—I suppose she was rewarded with food for such information, whether it was true or not—and after our meager lunch, two guards came and took me to sick bay. As punishment for something I didn't do, I had six good teeth pulled from my mouth by SS orderlies—without anesthetic.

I have never felt so alone, so friendless, and forsaken as I did in Ravensbrück where, during the last winter, there were 30-35,000 women living in a camp built for 10,000 and nowhere could I find a friend to trust, a friend who could give me the reassurance and encouragement I so desperately needed. One German woman I had made friends with at work in the factory asked me to write down a certain religious poem for her, so that she could look at it, remember the words, and gain strength from it. I felt warm knowing that I had contributed to her well being in this small way. When a guard caught her with it, she could have said she found it, but instead, she pointed me out. "Johanna wrote it and gave it to me." I was beaten. Another, time, someone accused me of stealing a piece of bread, even though the food in my hand was my own. I was locked in the bunker for three days with nothing to eat or drink. No effort was made to establish the truth, or to let me defend myself. But I found a great deal of comfort in the Lord, knowing that he was with me. Even without human friends, I didn't despair, but I longed for just a little companionship, for someone I could trust.

At school in Holland, everything I said or did was reported at home by my sister Ann, who was 16 months older. I had been only six months in the first grade when I was moved up to the second, becoming Ann's classmate. From that time through the seventh grade, I had a tattletale on my back. All year long, I looked forward to summer vacation, four weeks in August, when Mother had promised Grossvater that I could go to Germany to visit him.

Mother brought me to Amsterdam and Grossvater picked me up at the train depot in Berlin. The international railroad had special cars for women and Mother always asked one of the ladies to keep an eye on me, much to my dismay and chagrin. But what a joy to come to Berlin and see that big old man standing on the platform, leaning on his cane and searching the windows for my face. I started yelling as soon as I saw him and could hardly wait for the train to stop. He never picked me up to kiss me, nor bent down to my level, but as I threw my arms around him, he mussed my hair with his big hand, clearing his throat several times as I cried into his vest: "Oh, Grossvater, I am so happy to see you!"

"All right, all right. Calm down, now," he soothed gruffly. "We'll have a good time together." He was just like my mother in that he could not be demonstrative in his affection, but when he squeezed my hand, I knew that was his way of telling me, "I love you".

As soon as we reached the castle, off went my stockings and shoes. Somewhere, we found a pair of old pants and a shirt, and I was ready to check on the horses, greet all my dear friends, human and animal alike, and resume my position as Grossvater's right-hand man. I was only a girl when I had to be, for Mother, for I loved the special closeness of being a "guy" with Grossvater.

I remember one time the old housemaid, the only woman on the staff, brought me to Grossvater and complained about something I had done. I called her the gray lady because her hair, face, clothes, even her shoes were gray—and so was her attitude. Grossvater started slapping the arm of his chair, telling me how bad I was. I was really scared. I thought Grossvater would support me against the old crone, but here he was believing everything she said.

"All right, Miss Holthaus," Grossvater said. "You can go. I'll straighten her out." She sniffed and left, and I stood quietly in front of my stern grandfather, wondering what terrible punishment I was to face for the prank. "Come closer," Grossvater ordered me. I minced forward. "Closer. Here between my knees!" he thundered. Who would have dared disobey a roar like that. Then gently, very gently, he lifted my trembling chin with a thick finger, winked at me and said, "When will those old women learn to understand us guys?"

The four weeks of summer vacation passed too quickly for both of us, and when I had to leave for Holland, I was miserable. Coming home was no fun because my brothers and sisters resented the fact that they had not been allowed to go with me. If I had been smart, I would have kept quiet about my adventures during vacation, and saved myself some misery. Mother couldn't understand my relationship with Grossvater, and she oftened accused me of making up stories, since she couldn't believe the old count would spend so much time with a child, especially a "naughty" one like me. My brothers and sisters followed her disapproving lead, added to their resentment, and my homecoming was twice as bad as it might have been.

When I was 12, my oldest sister met me one winter day at school, something she had never done before. My scalp tingled with apprehension.

"Hurry home," she said abruptly. "Mother is leaving for Germany. Grandfather has died."

I ran home in a daze. Died, died, died. Please, no. Not Grossvater. Grossvater, Grossvater, please come and tell me it's not so. Dead means gone. Dead means I'll never see you again. Not dead, please, not dead.

He had been his usual robust self only four months earlier when I had been with him. He loved me and he would have told me if he felt sick. But Mother briskly explained that my hero, my friend, my precious, beloved Grossvater had suffered a stroke and died suddenly. I didn't even know what a stroke was. I only knew that I had to go to Germany, to the castle. Maybe there was something I could do that would stop the stroke, that would bring back my only friend.

I begged Mother to take me with her. She was incredulous. What business did I have traveling all that way for nothing. She did not understand; I could not explain the deep pain in my heart, the sorrow that engulfed me.

"At least bring me back something that he often touched," I pleaded, "like a button on his jacket." But Mother had no ear for my sentimental nonsense.

The next few days were spent in a bad dream world. I seriously thought of running away and trying to reach Germany. I could not cry. I could not be civil to my brothers and sisters; I neglected my homework and paid no attention in class. The unexpressed grief grew inside me, crowding my aching heart until I hurt so much I couldn't sleep. My eyes became dry and itchy from staring for long periods at nothing in particular, until finally I would remember to blink. Mother returned in 10 days. The next day, she took me into the living room that was used only on Sundays, or for formal occasions. She explained that Grossvater had left me the house and grounds where I had grown up. My uncle inherited the property in Juterbog, my aunt Gertrude, the family jewelry, my aunt Margaretha, the valuable paintings. Mother and my aunt Henrietta received stocks and bonds. Since I was only 12 years old, it had been decided that Mother's cousin Karl would manage the property for me until I was 18, when, according to the stipulations of the will, I could take over. Mother made it clear that there would be no more annual vacations to Germany by myself. If I wanted to go, I had to take the whole family with me. This seemed outrageous to me. How could she expect me to share my secret hiding places with them? The mountain, which wasn't more than a small hill, where I used to lie with butter on my face, trying to get a suntan. Or the big hole in the forest, which, according to Grossvater was the sleeping place of a bear family. There never seemed to be any bears around, but what did that matter, as long as I believed they were there?

I knew that I would no longer be allowed to go off by myself, or to ignore mealtimes. I wouldn't be able to go barefoot or wear old clothes. Maybe, too, I was afraid that one of my brothers or sisters might receive some of the attention and affection from the servants that had been entirely mine. The estate people had seen me grow up, watched my first steps, and cleansed my bleeding knees after a fall from a tree. They were my friends, mine alone, and I was very possessive of them. So I pretended to be indifferent to vacations in Germany, and year after year, we spent our summers at the beach, only seven miles from home.

At this time, I started a period of rebellion. A girl at school had told me that a widow could not have children. I knew that I was born two months after my father's death, and since we never had any sex education, I came to the conclusion that I was not Mother's real child. After all, why had I grown up far from the rest of the family? Why was I so different, why did I get spanked more than anyone else? I dared not ask Mother, but slowly I became convinced that I did not belong there with the others. I ran away several times, only to be caught and brought back within a few hours. I was unhappy and I took it out on anybody who happened to irritate me at the moment. I was also quite outspoken and didn't know when to keep my mouth shut, or when the truth should be shaded just a little. I apparently inherited that from my father. I remember a story that was often told about Father. He was on his way home from a business trip to Berlin and invited my uncle Hans to accompany him to Holland. Cousin Joe also wanted to come, but they didn't like him, so they left early in the morning. However, at a place where they had to change trains, Joe caught up with them. "What time did you leave?" Joe asked. "How come I didn't see you in Königsberg?" Hans kicked my father in an effort to warn him to keep his mouth shut, but Father said, "What's up, Hans? Why are you kicking me?" and told Joe the truth as to why he hadn't seen them. When they reached home, after a long, tiring journey, Father greeted Mother with a bear hug, cheerfully telling her, "We have two guests: one who is invited, and one who invited himself."

I was just as forthright and outspoken, but being a child, it made a big difference. Many times I repeated what I had heard Mother say to the manager of our store about people who had failed to pay their bills. When I got into one of my many fights with a neighbor's child, I would taunt, "You'd better tell your dad to take his business somewhere else, because we don't want him. He never pays his bills." Naturally, this always got back to our house, and I would be sent up to the guest room. Even though I pretended to be tough, I yearned for love and affection. But I couldn't bring myself to be sweet and lovable. I didn't dare talk back to Mother, but my facial expressions made words superfluous. In school, I was doing well in subjects like spelling, reading, composition, history and geography. But I hated math and science, and subsequently rebelled against those studies, making no effort to learn anything about them.

When I was almost 13 years old, our class was going to put on a play, which one of the Sisters had written. It was about five girls who, on their way to school, had to pass by a statue of the Madonna. One of the girls, who had recently lost her mother, poured out her sorrow and a miracle happened. The statue came to life and comforted the little girl. I desperately wanted to play the part of the Madonna, but I had no chance. I was a tomboy and obviously had neither the appearance nor the disposition required for that role. I hated the girl who was chosen. She was pretty, had blonde hair and a heart-shaped face. She was the pet of all the teachers and I was jealous of her every move.

I had an insignificant part to play as one of the children hopping and skipping around on the stage. On the evening of the performance, I waved a little peppershaker in front of the "statue" and the serene Madonna started sneezing. The audience roared with laughter and I was pleased beyond words. Nobody knew exactly what had happened, since their attention had not been on the dancing children, but the embarrassed and humiliated Madonna told the nuns later what had caused her to sneeze. That was the last straw. I was expelled from school. Mother realized then that I needed a stricter discipline and I was sent to a convent school far from my hometown. It took a full day of traveling to get there, on three different trains and a bus. Mother herself took me to the convent and told the Superior all about the problems I had created at home. There were about 50 girls in this school, which was on a high school level. I skipped the first grade level, and with some extra tutoring easily made it through the next four levels to graduation at the age of seventeen.

Life in the convent school was boring. There was a far stricter regimen than even my mother's stifling house rules: no talking in the halls; talking only in the dining room after the supervising nun gave permission; beds made in a certain way at a certain time; full school uniforms worn; and marching in formation to the chapel, classroom or elsewhere. We weren't allowed to keep any money or jewelry. If one of the girls received a parcel containing sweets, it had to be turned in, and then evenly distributed among all the girls on the next Sunday, "goodie day". The nuns were so afraid that we would commit a sin that they warned us about things we were not yet aware of. In Holland, we usually linked arms, but this was strictly forbidden. If two girls were seen talking and walking together, they were told to join the group. Any expression of affection was severely frowned upon. There was a whole system of spying and informing. Every girl had her favorite Sister, and there was a lot of competition for the nuns' attention.

We had Easter, summer and Christmas vacations, but only on the first Sunday of the month could we have visitors. I was there four years and Mother came just once. Scarlet fever attacked the convent when I was 14 and we were all sent home for two weeks so that the building could be fumigated. I had a train ticket to Amsterdam where one of my brothers was supposed to meet me and take me home. But when I arrived in the capital, no one was there to greet me. I had no money; I couldn't go on. What was I to do? My oldest sister was engaged at that time to a man from Amsterdam, I recalled, and set out to find his office. But I arrived there only to learn he was on vacation in my hometown. I was given his mother's address, but she too was gone.

My sister's fiancé had a colleague whom I secretly admired. He was also on vacation, but hadn't left yet to go to my mother's to join his friend. Once I found him, he promised to take me home, leaving me at a restaurant while he went to the barbershop. There were only businessmen in the cafe, and I felt completely out of place and unsophisticated in my dull school uniform. But when my friend returned, he had bought me a bag of chocolate candy, and I was convinced that he was in love with me. Had I not read that young men brought candy or flowers to their girlfriends? At the ticket window, he bought two first class tickets. I had never been in the elite compartment. Then he purchased a magazine—the nuns had warned us about reading such works of the devil. What more proof of his love did I need? I was on Cloud Nine and wished the trip would last 45 long hours instead of the 45 minutes it actually took. Mother wasn't at home when we arrived, and my sister told me that the best way to get rid of the scarlet fever germs was to take a long walk in freezing weather. She sent me with a message to our seamstress, who lived five miles out of town. Coming into the house, exhausted and ice cold, I was quietly hanging my coat in the hall closet when I heard my sister say to my new love, "Bert, how could you buy my little sister this kind of magazine?" My heart shattered when I heard him reply, "Well, I didn't know what to talk about with the kid." I promised myself I would never fall in love again. Enough of dreaming.

Back in Ravensbrück...

After I started working in the Siemens factory, I was moved to Barracks No. 3. Barracks No. 1 through No. 3 were the "good" barracks, because the people in them were relatively clean. There were women who saw to it that we washed regularly, with cold water, of course, and one woman who checked everybody for lice. Another woman did nothing but clean the barracks. And most of the women had the better, cleaner jobs, like working in sickbay, administration or the factory. In Barracks No. 1 were the Polish women who worked in the kitchen, thanks to the Polish kitchen foreman. In my barracks, the third one, most of the women worked in sickbay. Here I found many intelligent, formally educated women with whom I could talk at length about many subjects. The blockova was Communist, as many of the blockovas were, and I often found myself in heated arguments with her or one of her comrades, I felt so strongly about Catholicism. We tried to show each other why one way of living was better than the other.

The Communists told me that religion was the opium of the people—I think it was Lenin who first said that—but I argued that the need for a god is implanted in all men. Wherever you go, whether Europe, America or to a tribe in the darkest part of Africa, people will be expressing the need to believe in a higher being, a higher power, whether they worship the God I do, or another god in the form of a tree or a cow. The Catholic Church was trying to keep its people uninformed, the Communists argued, lying to them and keeping them ignorant of reality. "Then tell me why the church sends out missionaries to teach the people," I told them. "In the Middle Ages, it was just the Church that brought education to the people. There were no teachers but the monks, who wrote down everything and held classes every day." They laughed at me, they made fun of me, and I have to admit that many of them were quite persuasive in their arguments. But by then my belief and faith in God were firm. I had to respect them for their intelligence, though, and when the Communists got food parcels, they shared with the rest. Not many Christians in the camp did that, and the Jehovah's Witnesses did so only in exchange for a commitment.

It was in Barracks No. 3, too, that I first began receiving letters again from my mother, and we were allowed to receive food parcels. The months-old letters were in pencil and censored by the Nazis; the food packages were gone through and articles removed. Still, it was heaven to hear from the outside world, to know that my mother and son were still alive, and waiting for me to come home.

There were lots of Russian prisoners, not only those who had been in the Red Army, but the Germans sent thousands of Russian women to Germany after conquering Russian villages, forcing the foreigners to work in the factories that kept the Nazi war machine going. When those girls missed work for a few days without a good excuse, they were sent to concentration camps and put to work there. We were cheap labor for the Nazis. For example, the Siemens company paid three and one half marks per day per prisoner to the camp, but we didn't cost the camp even half a mark. There were about 3000 women working in the tailor shops making uniforms. If you didn't make your quota, they deducted food from your ration. So there were some women who worked twice as hard as necessary, fearful of losing their meager food portions, and then the others couldn't keep up. The hard workers then got the slower workers' rations. It was kill or be killed, let someone else go without food or starve yourself.

But still, we had light moments. I used to recite comical poems I had learned as a child. When I first came, my appearance greatly added to my stand-up comedian role. I had no hair, and big frame glasses loomed in front of my thin, drawn face. I was given a dress without a belt, which made a nice tent for me to walk within, and wide-legged pants that had ribbons for tying in front and in back. They were woolen, scratchy and hot during the summer, and reached just below my knee, ending in a loose cuff: red and green and blue checkered. I would get up on a table and dance, flapping the skirt up to show the checkered bloomers, singing a nonsensical tune all the while. They would laugh and say, "Oh, you are so crazy." And I laughed back, boasting, "Yes, I know, but as long as I know I'm crazy, I'm not dangerous. Your trouble is that you don't know that you're just as crazy as I am."

Once we had a few Russian girls who danced for us. The others sang and the Russians danced to the music of the combined voices, sitting on their haunches with arms folded, kicking their legs out in a dance I had never seen before. But the best singers in the camp were the gypsies. In the summer evenings, they would sit outside their barracks, singing and brushing their long, black wavy hair. I couldn't understand the words, they might have been Hungarian, but the melodies were beautiful.

Maria, Nadia, Katje and Freda were four Russian girls with whom I worked in the Siemens factory. They never got packages or heard from their families. Katje was retarded and didn't even know the name of the village where she used to live. She had to count little lids or screws or bolts as her job, but she couldn't count any further than ten, so when she counted as high as ten, she wrote down a check mark, then started counting again. Whenever I got a package from home, I would share the contents with the four girls. In appreciation, they would often dance and sing for me. Their voices were not so good—especially Maria's, which was loud and screechy, but it was still a nice gesture. Because of this special relationship, they invited me to their barracks for Christmas, my first in Ravensbrück, and my second since I was arrested. I gave them the small gift I had brought with me, then blinked back the tears as I saw what they had prepared for me.

Those girls, who never got any food packages, had saved bread from their rations, slicing it thinly and topping it with the slightest golden moisture of margarine. This was a treat as we got only one small square per week. Another slice of bread had some marmalade on it; we got one tablespoon each week; a third, something small and green that I hoped was a bit of parsley. All of this was served on a piece of cardboard, and it was a feast meant only for me.

"Come, let's eat together," I urged. "No," they insisted, they couldn't hold another bite, they had already had plenty. I took a small bite and the morsel almost stuck in my dry throat. I saw their eyes go from the plate to my mouth as I took each bite. When I looked up, they looked away. When I tried to offer some to them, they were indignant. This sacrifice was for me, to show their love and friendship. The bland, lumpy marmalade became like nectar; the dry, crumbling bread, a French delicacy; I basked in the warmth of this unexpected affection.

CHAPTER SEVEN

The Camp at its Worst

Some of the women in Ravensbrück had been there since 1933. Imprisonment was an established way of life; freedom a forgotten privilege; social castes rigidly formed. The stark barracks, badly prepared food, confining stone walls and absence of even the smallest personal luxury no longer figured as deprivation. Things were as they had to be, and only organized strength—for good or bad—could change the order of life in the camp.

Our single-width beds were stacked three high in the dark green wooden barracks. I always somehow got the top bunk in my various living quarters, but when I came, there were no beds at all available and I slept on an upside-down table, using my clothing as a pillow. I thought that was bad until I shared a bunk with the woman who put urine on her bald head: better a hard plank than straw-filled bedding that reeked and crawled. A single bulb in the ceiling of the barracks never provided enough light to identify the parts of your bedding that were mobile, and later on, even that light was removed.

To the right of the large gate that served the camp as both exit and entrance was a small hut for guards. A dining room for SS personnel was to the left. Around a big open square stood the guard building, bath hall and kitchen, the office for the head of the women guards. They looked real smart in their gray uniforms with high polish black boots like the men wore. In Germany during the war, everyone had to work and many women didn't want to be put through the drudgery and hard labor of a factory, so they thought they would join the SS, wear a flashy uniform, and spend a lot of time with the choice males of the SS. But they were in for a big disappointment. Those who worked in camps like Ravensbrück had to get up very early to be ready for roll call, and then they spent most of the day with smelly, disease-ridden, lice-infested sub-humans—us.

Sickbay was at the upper end of the lager strasse—camp street—with the barracks situated on side streets, which intersected the main artery. Then there was the building where luggage was stored and where the work was divided. At the end of the lager strasse, and to the left, was the punishment barracks, the prison within the prison. Once a prisoner from the punishment barracks escaped, and all the people in that barracks had to stand roll call the entire night, while the guards looked for the woman. When they found her, instead of punishing her with a beating, the Kommandant gave her over to the sleepless prisoners in the barracks she escaped from. Within ten minutes, the woman was dead.

Behind that barracks, another wide street stretched, with more barracks in orderly formation like big, green world-weary soldiers. Neat, weeded, bordered beds of tiny flowers lined all the buildings as evidence to visitors that the Nazis were going to great lengths to make their guests as comfortable as possible during this misfortunate interlude. But some of the carefully nurtured falsehoods took root only to grow pale and spindly in the shadow of the high stone wall that held captive the filthy, rapacious beast called Ravensbrück. Capillaries of electricity in the form of barbed wire stretched from the transformers on top of the wall, creating a foreboding no man's land within the triangle of wire, stone and bare ground. Three or four times during the three years I spent in Ravensbrück, women threw themselves onto the wire, no longer able to contend with their empty lives. Escapes were seldom attempted. Only once in 10 years did anyone successfully escape: a Polish woman who got to England by way of the underground. The woman she escaped with was discovered hiding in Warsaw when the Germans were withdrawing. The German people were so afraid of the Gestapo and SS that when an escapee came to them for help, the good citizens immediately notified the camp.

The first punishment for a recaptured escapee was to have her head shaved. Then she received 25 strokes from a two-by four-

The Camp at its Worst

inch board. The day I was sent to the bunker for supposedly stealing a piece of bread, I saw a girl with her head shaved, big tears spilling over her pale cheeks, her eyes blank. A second girl was taken into a room and made to bend over a big log, her arms, legs and torso strapped down by leather bands. As the doctor and bunker commander looked on, a second prisoner—either asocial or criminal (they volunteered for such duty) beat the escapee, who had to count aloud as the strokes mounted to 25. After the beating, the escapee was sentenced to six months in the punishment barracks. There, no one was allowed contact with anyone else in the camp. The women had little free time, working from early morning until long after dark, unloading barges in the nearby canal. They were often too tired to sleep; too tense to relax, and they were given only half of the inadequate food ration we received.

I never entertained the idea of escaping. I knew I could never make it, and the threat of the punishment barracks was more than enough incentive to keep me inside the wall. Many of the women in that barracks were lesbian. Homosexuals were severely punished in Germany, and during that time, the offenders were placed in the camps. How ironic to put them in a prison that, because of overcrowding, had up to five women sharing two beds. Any political prisoner who wasn't lesbian and had been put in the special barracks for some other offense endured degrading physical attacks or died defending herself. The guards were never concerned over the death of a prisoner, regardless of how she died. It was just one less body they had to account for.

The bunker—jail for prisoners who committed lesser crimes—was the only stone building in camp, placed behind the administrative offices. A tailor's shop for making uniforms was inside the wall. Outside were towers for guards, and little bunkers along the road to the Siemens factory that were manned by soldiers during air raids. In peacetime, the Siemens company had manufactured phones and radios. Operated by concentration camp inmates, and relocated, the factory now supplied parts for planes and submarines.

It was 1943 and the Battle of Stalingrad was history. The "erasing" of the Warsaw ghetto began in April, with the Jewish Combat Organization fighting back every bloody minute of 28 days. Mussolini resigned in July, and the anti-Nazi Badoglio took his place. Italy surrendered to the Allies in September, declaring war on Germany in October.

We were pretty well aware of the way the war was going as we fought our own battles for survival inside the camp. The Nazi newspaper—Völkischer Beobachter—was allowed inside the camp, and in the knitting room one woman read aloud to the others as they worked on clothing for the troops. Then each of these women would pass the news along until the entire camp was aware of the latest victory or defeat. Of course, we had to read between the lines in the reports of Nazi defeat, or allow for exaggeration of a Nazi victory, but it wasn't difficult to comprehend the real situation when the cover-up was so obvious: "According to plan, our troops withdrew victoriously", was one way of explaining victory for the Allies. Knowing the end of Nazi rule was at least in sight helped make our incarceration a little more bearable.

The beautiful Viennese who acted as our blockova in Barracks No. 3, Resi, was a woman of high ideals, a Communist. In that barracks, a lot of the women were Czech, and in that country, Communism is predominant among the intelligentsia. I was never a great politician, but it seemed to me that both Communism and Nazism were totalitarian dictatorships: they both tried to break up the family, wanting people to live only for the State or the Reich, and they suppressed all church activity. There were many Communists in the camp who were idealists like Resi. They were good people who would often go hungry in order to give their small ration of food to someone who seemed to need it more. Yet I could not leave their statements unchallenged, even though I respected these women on a personal level. I wasn't the only one who argued against Communism, but perhaps I was the most outspoken, because of my strong belief in God and my Catholic faith. I knew that I couldn't have lived long enough to be arguing with them if God hadn't helped me stay sane and survive Nürnberg's tortures and Rothenfeld's hard labor and starvation. My brother had been ordained a priest in February of that year and Mother wrote me that he had obtained special permission from the Nazis to leave his home in France and spend two days in Holland with his family. He said a Low Mass (one without song and organ music) the first morning in his mother country, in the chapel of a nursing home. It was offered for the whole family. My mother had sent wires to all her other children and they arrived later in the day. The next morning, my brother, the newly ordained priest, said his second mass, a High Mass, for me. Each time I was beaten, when I almost let go of my will to survive, I thought of that mass, and determined that it was not for nothing.

Just when things would almost reach the breaking point, it seemed that something good, something light-hearted would happen to take me out of my black mood. Once we even had a wedding. The bride was already engaged when she was taken prisoner, and her fiancé was being sent to the Front as a soldier, so they wanted to be married before he left. He came to Ravensbrück and their wedding was held in the administration building directly outside the camp. When the bride came back from the ceremony, the women in her barracks had prepared a bridal bed for her—a hand-embroidered pillow case sacrificed by some soft-hearted pilferer, surrounded by pansies from the camp flower beds. Handmade gifts came from women in other parts of the camp. Many of them were accomplished artists and they used severely limited resources to create things of beauty, which were even more precious in the ugly darkness of the lives we led. Intricately patterned curtains were made out of salvaged bits of paper; toothbrushes became leaping horses or stately swans; threads pulled from old, soiled cloth were reshaped in the most intricate needlework.

I remembered other weddings...

My sister married not long after I enrolled in the convent school, when I was about 14, and I got special permission to leave school and attend the wedding. It was a crowded, festive occasion and I fully appreciated the color and gaiety, laughter and camaraderie after months of black and white discipline. Most of the day, I was right next to Mother, or well within her sight, but at dinner, Mother sat with the bridal couple and I was shunted off to the other end of the long table. It had been a long time since lunch and I was hungry, but the formal eight-course meal started with light appetizers and proceeded slowly. A different wine was served with each course, and I drank mine along with the adults, helping myself to the bottles that the waiters left on the table. I had never tasted wine or liquor, and I wondered what people liked in the reds and whites that ranged from lip-puckering bitter to throat-gagging sweet. Then we came to a little French white wine called Bergerac that tasted like a carbonated soft drink, and I had emptied my goblet a number of times before a relative noticed that something was wrong. I was dead drunk.

Six months later when my oldest brother married, I was not allowed to go home for the ceremony. I couldn't believe my mother's handwriting—I read the letter a second time. Everyone would be home and having a great time, except for me, the black sheep. My mind flashed back to my sister's wedding day, and I mentally winced at the picture of myself lying in bed vomiting on myself as my horrified mother and sisters looked on in shock. I stubbornly jutted out my chin in opposition to the tears that quivered at the edges of my eyes. I would never go home again. If they didn't want to see me, if they were so scandalized, then I would oblige them by disappearing without a trace. Perhaps I would get sick and die. Then let them moan and cry and wish they had treated me decently. Or if I didn't die, at least I would cease my flow of weekly letters. They could worry their heads off—what did I care?

Five big decorated cakes, accompanied by boxes of soft drinks, arrived at the convent the day of the wedding. As compensation for missing the real event, Mother was providing the makings for a surrogate wedding celebration, making me a proxy bride, or at least the hostess of a farce. We marched into the dining room and the girls gasped at the sight of the rose-bedecked cakes, but I lost my head, grabbed the first cake and hurled it against the wall. Immediately, I was overpowered by nuns and dragged into a classroom. I pounded on the locked door, my frustration and anger mounting as the sound of chattering, cake-devouring schoolgirls penetrated the walls of my makeshift prison. I threw myself into a chair, short breaths bursting through clenched teeth.

One of the nuns unlocked the door and stepped quietly inside. I couldn't look at her to see who it was, but stared malevolently at the desk in front of me. She stopped beside my chair and gently touched the top of my head, her fingers stroking a few displaced hairs back into smoothness. Some hardness inside me cracked and burst, and I cried as I rarely had before. She said nothing for a long time. She just stood there, patting my head and waiting for the years of saved-up grief to wash away as I thought of every unkind word or thoughtless deed I had suffered. At last my tears subsided and with gasps of breath, hiccoughs and a sleeve across my wet face, I began to regain my composure. The sister brought me a glass of water and pulled up a chair. She began to talk, telling me of her childhood, the little garden behind her parents' house and the kitten she buried there. She spoke of many things, but not at all of my brother's wedding or my bad behavior. All along, she stroked my hair. The comfort of her closeness, the warmth of her hand and the quiet firmness of her voice reassured me and I relaxed. I was exhausted, as if I had run a terrible distance, and I followed willingly as she led me to my bed.

The Camp at its Worst 79

I slept from early evening through the long dark night, and in the morning life continued as usual. Nobody mentioned the incident. I continued writing my weekly letters and when summer came I did not remember my vow to never go home. I finished high school and the principal erased my mother's vague ambitions for me to go into law, encouraging me instead to develop my flair for languages, which resulted in my enrollment at the university in Breslau to study German.

My high school report cards were heavy as lead on one side with perfect grades in Dutch, Latin, English, French and German, "B" marks in history and geography, but goose down light on the other side with "D"s and even "E"s in math, geometry and chemistry. The principal referred to it as my downhill slide. But I graduated at 17, the youngest in my class. We traveled to Amsterdam for the oral final exam and we were given the results at once. I was so relieved and proud to have my diploma in my hands that I called Mother on the phone to give her the good news.

"Of course, you made it," she said flatly. "You'd better have. Do you have to call me long distance for that?"

The recollection of these events was like a transfusion of new life for me.

Back to camp...

Every three months, each blockova was required to ask the women in her block for volunteer prostitutes. The men who worked in the isolated concentration camps needed a woman now and then, the Nazis reasoned, so anyone who worked extra hard could earn tickets with which to purchase a few minutes of feminine charm. Any woman who volunteered (I'm proud to say none of the political prisoners ever did) got good food, a sun lamp and nice clothes for a six-month stay. When they fulfilled their service contract, they returned to the barracks with suitcases full of candy, cigarettes and lingerie from their customers. Then they were released to go home. Someone went home every day, even without gaining his or her freedom through prostitution. Not everybody was there for the rest of their lives. I don't know if any of those freed women tried to help the rest of us by making the public aware of our dilemma.

Resi, our blockova, hated asking for volunteers for this disgusting service. She would come in fuming and blurt out, "You know what I have come to ask. What I must ask every three months. I can't get it out of my mouth. Who? Who wants to?"

There were many older women in Barracks 3, including 72-year-old Mutti Behreiter, Little Mother, who had been in Ravensbrück since 1935 because she was a Communist. We would roar with laughter when she tottered forward every three months to eagerly deliver her best line: "Resi, I would like to. I will volunteer."

Two other senior barracks mates, Frau Puff and Frau Rentmeister, were camp police. The old ladies patrolled at night, sleeping during the day. Their job was not hard at all, because everyone was afraid to leave the barracks at night, since often the SS went about with police dogs. In fact, the two tiny crones spent most of their police duty time stealing loot from the building where our food packages from home were kept.

Filth was one of the hardest parts of being in Ravensbrück. There was no toilet paper, no sanitary napkins or cloths for those few women whose menstrual cycles continued after months or years of constant starvation and mental duress. A change of clothes happened very seldom, and you had to get awfully dirty before the blockova could petition for clean apparel. We tried to keep ourselves clean, but with no soap, only cold water, and a twelve by eighteen inch hand towel, it was an uphill battle. Every six weeks we were told we were getting clean towels and would be ordered to turn in our soiled ones. After we had thrown the stiff, smelly rectangles into a pile with hundreds of others, sometimes a counter order came through: no fresh towels. Now which towel is mine?

And after I left Barracks 3 and came to Barracks 5 and 17, I got lice. Lice and Krätze—scabies—were a constant threat to our health. The scabies rash spread like wildfire through Ravensbrück, and though not all of us were infected—I was one of the lucky ones—everyone in camp had to report barrack by barrack to sickbay. We undressed completely, then shuffled by in front of two or three doctors. Some of the women pirouetted for inspection as if they were on stage, while others, like nuns, were ashamed and embarrassed, even after all this time of performing the most private acts before dozens of eyes. We often had to stand stark naked in front of men, both guards and doctors, though the guards usually moved back and forth unseeingly. After all, we weren't much to look at, even as naked females. When we were deloused, we were herded out of the barracks, leaving our clothing behind, and stood outside naked in all kinds of weather. Since the buildings and our garments weren't always fumigated thoroughly, it wasn't long before the lice took over again.

Sickbay was one place we avoided whenever possible. The general opinion was that if you weren't sick when you went there, you certainly would be afterwards. I observed one woman who stood in line for a long time to get treatment for an ugly sore on her hand that had worms crawling around in it. When she finally reached the medication point, the head nurse was sickened by the sight of the prisoner's hand, and called her dirty names, kicking her and sending her away without help. It didn't do much good to get medical treatment, anyway. The bandages were thin as toilet paper, and the fine dirt we walked in was like coal dust, made powdery by thousands of dragging feet, seeping into wounds and beginning infections that often led to death in a matter of days. Though we in Barracks 3 went to great lengths to keep our bodies, clothing and living quarters as clean as possible, many women never washed themselves or their clothing, manifesting an almost palpable odor of dried urine, excrement and blood.

Unless our squalidness threatened the health of our captors, as in the case of lice and scabies, cleanliness was never encouraged, except perhaps as a means of punishment, like when I was made to clean latrines for a week. The guard who gave me the assignment thought she would really bring me to my knees, but I was determined to make the best of it. When she came to gloat over my suffering, I was singing and mopping the floor, walking backwards and pretending not to have heard her come in, until at last I backed right into her, swinging the wet, slimy mop against her legs as I turned in mock surprise. Anytime I was punished or tortured, I told myself: "They can do nothing to me without God's will. If He doesn't want me to be beaten, this person's arm will be paralyzed the moment he tries to strike me. If God lets him beat me, then there is a reason, a lesson to be learned."

By then, I had come so far, been through so much, that I had given myself over totally to God. I very seldom lost courage because I knew that my mother and my brother, who was a priest, would be praying for me each day. I knew that I had a son who needed me and who expected me to come home. I felt very close to Christ all that time, talking with Him, knowing that He walked beside me through the foulness of Ravensbrück. "I cannot do it alone," I told Him many times. "You must be my travel companion constantly, if I am to survive." All around me, there were those who weren't surviving. There was Maria, a Russian surgeon who had been with the Red Army. She worked in sickbay, and the Nazi doctors worked beside her to learn from her. There was a room there that was reserved for the dying, usually sufferers from typhoid fever, and Maria hid another in that room, a Russian, an opera singer whose nerves hadn't held. One fall morning we stood in formation for roll call, the sky a brilliant blue and the sun shining above our heads and the stone walls of the camp, as the warming earth revolved and basked in the warmth of the sun. The stillness was broken only by a tremulous voice from a window in the end of sick bay as the demented Russian singer rejoiced in the magnificence of a glorious day, and caroled her way to death. She and Maria both disappeared that day.

Then two English women were dropped behind enemy lines to do intelligence work. They were captured and brought to Ravensbrück to await an execution order from Berlin. Early one morning just before the 4:45 roll call, two SS men came and got the spies. We were standing outside in our rows of ten when we heard the shots and knew that the girls were dead. For a moment there was silence, as if every woman were holding her breath. Then somewhere in the lines a defiant, tearful sound broke the stillness as one woman, and then another, and another began singing "Nearer My God to Thee". In English, in German, in Dutch and French, the words tumbled out in tribute to the young women's bravery, even as the SS beat us with their rubber batons, we sang it through to the end.

CHAPTER EIGHT

The Warsaw Loot Place

Ravensbrück is known for its medical experiments on the women interned there. The prisoners were guinea pigs, or rabbits, as we called them, for doctors who thought of them only as animals, not as humans, with rights or feelings. Not far from the main women's camp was a little camp for men. These male prisoners were placed in a freezing liquid—I don't know if it was water—to see how cold a human being could get before it killed him. When the naked man was brought out of the solution, a woman prisoner was forced to disrobe and "warm him up" while the experimenters timed the process to see how long it took to get the man's blood circulating again. There was a Dr. Treitel (camp gossip said that he had a German father, but an English mother) who was a general practitioner and wanted to learn surgery. He started his training by removing goiters from female prisoners. The doctor operated on seven women before he perfected his surgery. The eighth patient survived. Although seven human beings had died under his knife, he, at last, had mastered the process and the German medical field had gained a trained surgeon.

A Dr. Rosenthal—it sounds like a Jewish name, but he was an SS doctor—had a relationship with one of the Ravensbrück inmates and made her pregnant. It was evidently a voluntary situation on her part because another strict rule in the camp was that none of the men could touch us. The Kommandant was very severe in that respect, and we had only to complain once. According to the camp grapevine, the girl was a German political prisoner and he impregnated her, and then aborted her, five times. When this was at last discovered by the Kommandant, the doctor was sentenced to six years hard labor, his lover to eight years. But before they could start their sentences, the Russians came and the camp was liberated.

Calf muscles were removed from the legs of Polish women from Barracks 15 and transplanted in the legs of soldiers on the Front. One day during roll call, five of these women were told to report to sick bay the following Monday for operations. All of the women refused, saying, "Kill us if you must, but we are not rabbits." The SS guards locked the five women in the bunker, shutting the other Poles in their quarters, sealing the doors and shutters for three days. There was enough food in the packages sent from home to keep the women from getting too hungry, but the lack of oxygen weakened many of them and they fainted when they were at last released and forced to stand for roll call.

That Monday was dark and overcast, as if nature mourned with us. The five who dared to defy the SS orders were operated on in a dim room without sterile instruments and without anesthetics. Throughout the camp, women walked sadly without speaking, their heads bowed, lips moving in prayer. The animal screams from the bunker pierced our ears as seconds dragged by like lifetimes, and even after the sounds had faded and gone, the pain hung in the air, and the moans echoed through the night.

The Allies invaded France in June 1944, the same month a flying bomb landed on Hitler's bunker and the Russians started on their way to Poland. Another attempt on the Führer's life was made in July. The flow of mail between Germany and other countries stopped about then, and I knew nothing further of my mother and son.

I purposely broke my eyeglasses in order to be transferred from the Siemens factory in the fall of 1944. My job there was to dip small parts in a liquid metal and then in a hot bath, and the resultant fumes burned my eyes and caused me to cough incessantly. I was afraid that I would get tuberculosis or something else, and used the broken glasses as an excuse for not being able to continue the work. A girl from my block was clerk in Work Division and she obtained a position for me in Bekleidungswerk 1,

The Warsaw Loot Place

what we called the Warsaw Loot Place. It was a depot for all the belongings confiscated from the Jews and other "enemies" of the Reich.

I stole what I could. I went to work in the morning wearing only a dress, no pants or undershirt, and a short jacket. When I came home in the evening, I could hardly move because of all the clothes I had on beneath my dress. The belongings of displaced Europeans and transported Jews came in by the trainload. We unloaded everything from silverware and lingerie to books, chess games; there was even a grand piano.

Working in Bekleidungswerk 1 saved my life and gave me a chance to help others. The clothing and toilet articles, as well as medicine now and then, could be traded for sugar, bread or margarine, which had likewise been stolen. I managed to find working positions for 20 of my friends, once I was put in charge. For those friends I could not help otherwise, I stole combs, toothbrushes and paste, or face cream—items they longed for. To steal was to "organize", according to camp vernacular, and the French women came to call me La Chef d' Organisation—The Head Thief.

I have never had a nightgown as beautiful as the one I organized in Ravensbrück: flowing green crepe georgette. We had neither food for the living nor caskets for the dead, but the depot overflowed with dishes, crystal, silver, candles and artwork; linens bearing the crests of noble families; tuxedos and evening gowns. There was a complete set-up for a dental office, from patient's chair right down to the last dental tool.

Six hundred women from Belgium and Holland arrived in September, coming from a concentration camp in Holland. Someone came into the barracks and announced the arrival of the Dutch women, so I went out to watch them come in. They walked five abreast, wearing long blue coveralls and carrying overnight bags, packages and rolled woolen blankets. They were the absolute picture of health, compared to us, but I knew it wouldn't last long, and I knew they wouldn't be allowed to keep what they had. I couldn't approach them directly, but I walked alongside the group, staring straight ahead and talking rapidly in Dutch. "Eat everything you have. They are going to take it all. Eat! As much as you can. They won't let you have a single thing."

Word passed through the ranks, and the sweat of fear rolled down their faces, their eyes darted quickly from side to side. One after the other, the women passed things to me, pleading, beseeching, "I beg of you, just take this small thing. Keep it for me, please."

"I am in Barracks 3, my name is Johanna and you can come get it tomorrow," I repeated hurriedly. I went back and forth between the square full of milling newcomers and my nearby barracks, carrying and stashing all sorts of valuables—in particular, medicines, vitamins, cod liver oil and Scott's emulsion. When the women filtered in during the next few days, they were full of gratitude since full realization of their other losses had registered, and many of them gave me part of their treasure as thanks.

The Dutch and Belgians had not been at all prepared for Ravensbrück. In the camp in Holland that they had just left, the prisoners had sometimes thrown food away; they had so much to eat from Red Cross supplies. And many of them had relatives or friends who lived nearby, in addition to the friendly neighboring country people who brought fresh food each day. We Ravensbrück veterans had become acclimatized to the slow starvation, adjusting over a long period of time to the ever decreasing supply and quality of our food. When I first arrived in camp, we got a chunk of bread at supper time that was big enough to be split and part held over for breakfast the next day. During the last winter, we were reduced to feeling grateful for the thin, hard slice we got once a day. These 600 women came from an abundance of fresh wholesome vegetables and bread to nearly nothing at all. The shock to their systems was severe. Many of them died, not only from starvation, but also from their state of mind, it seemed. Most of them, full of recent news of the war and sure the Allies were just over the next hill, were convinced that they would be home for Christmas. When three months of optimism brought them only further into misery, the dank emptiness of the holy day was more than they could face. They let go of the one hope that was holding their heads above water.

There weren't enough uniforms to outfit the trainload of new prisoners, so the Nazis took the suitcases in the depot—many of them belonging to those of us already there, not just Warsaw loot—and emptied them, giving the clothing to the women who just arrived. But to identify those in civilian clothing as KZ inmates, the Nazis painted big white crosses on the backs of the dresses and coats. Or sometimes they cut a cross from other material and sewed it on the outer garment. I organized a beautiful, highly fashionable full-length coat that winter. To keep attention from my new attire, I used chalk to draw a white cross on the back, which, at a distance, looked like "official" white paint on the dark blue field. Along with the coat, I stole a pair of suede shoes. If anyone approached me about my numerous acquisitions, I could always say, "My mother sent that to me. If you don't believe me, just ask them at the Effectenkamer. They will tell you." That was the depot where prisoners' suitcases and parcels were stored. With nearly 35,000 women in the camp, such a statement could hardly be verified. In truth, the only clothing that got through to me from my mother was an old bathrobe I had left at home in Holland.

One day there came a whole train full of shoes, not in boxes. or paired, just thrown loose into the railroad cars. We had to throw them out of the train onto the ground, then pick the lot of them up and pack them into the Warsaw Loot Place to sort them. The SS themselves weren't allowed to take anything from this place, not if it was worth more than 10 marks, and they were punished for such theft. Still, there were those who tried. A soldier came in with a requisition for underwear for the troops, spied a newly-sorted pile of women's shoes, and asked if I had a pair to fit his wife—he knew her size.

"You know that I'm not allowed to give anything here. I'll be beaten if I'm caught."

"But I'll give you anything you want," he insisted. "If you want a cigarette, a whole package of cigarettes, I will trade for the shoes."

I was in no mood to argue with a determined Nazi soldier, and I knew I could do some lucrative trading myself with a whole package. I didn't smoke, but I knew plenty of women who were more than eager to trade an entire day's bread ration for just one cigarette.

A supervisor stepped in the door of the sorting room just as the soldier turned from the shoe table, a pair of dainty black pumps in his hands.

"Kommensie her! Where do you think you're going with those shoes?"

The soldier pointed a finger at me, a glass wall of determination sliding down over his features. "This woman gave them to me. She insisted I take them. I was just going to..."

"You dirty liar! You know darned well I told you I am not allowed to let anyone have anything without submitting a requisition form." I yelled and called him more names, barging around the end of the counter to get right up in his face—I figured I should take the offensive.

He sputtered and cringed before my unexpected tirade, which ended only when the supervisor told us both to shut up.

"Halt's Maul! Enough of this!" He ordered the soldier to return the shoes to their place, lecturing him all the while, and continuing to berate him as the young man marched stiffly across the room and out the door.

And I still had 20 little tobacco-filled gold mines.

One certain officer came almost every week with requisitions to furnish a home for officers that was near the camp. He could choose whatever he wished to have in the way of furnishings, and picked out several Oriental rugs for the house. But he was a collector of Oriental carpets himself, and he asked me for a little one that would not be included on the inventory. Bacon and eggs proved to be more than a tempting offer. Middle-aged, he was SS, but he was also anti-Nazi, or so I believed from the short conversations we had had. On that intuitive feeling, I had based a liking for the man. He would have to trust me not to report him, just as I would have to trust him to bring me the promised booty.

I've never had such a reward for a risk taken as the greasy sweet pork and twin boiled ovals that came to me the following week. My eyes reveled in the smooth whiteness of the peeled eggs; the way my fingers pressed into the skin was like caressing and squeezing a measure of silk. The blue tinted pearls broke open to reveal powdery gray-gold centers. My nostrils flared at the heavy scent of the seasoned bacon, and I tore into the meat—something I had been without for so very long. There were times that non-descript chunks of something appeared in our watery soup, but I was never sure it was really meat, nor did I want to know its origin.

Every night we marched from Bekleidungswerk to the camp— it took about 15 minutes—after submitting to a search at the depot exit. Sometimes I asked the guards, "You want me to help search? It will go much faster." And they were always tired and impatient to get off duty, so they would say to each other, "Sure. Why not? It can only be of help to us."

Then I would turn to the women lining up before us and say sternly in French, "All who have taken something, come to me to be searched, but look serious. Don't give us away." And if a guard asked me to translate, I would paraphrase, in case she could understand a little of the language, "I told them all who have stolen something, throw it away before you are searched by me, because I search seriously."

Other times, I could pretend to be busy finishing up my work until the groups of searched and unsearched workers had grown enough to nearly overlap. Then I went quietly to stand with those who had passed inspection.

We had no medicine inside Ravensbrück, so when a suitcase filled entirely with medical supplies opened beneath my hands; I could hardly believe what I saw. My thoughts were immediately of the importance of getting some of it back to the prison—but how?

Shortly before that time, I had organized a pair of gloves with high, wide cuffs like the motorcyclists have. They would be ideal to hide pills from a routine search, I told myself, and managed to get most of the contents of a 600-tablet aspirin bottle into the big mittens. Nobody even eyed my hands as we filed out of the depot, and I rewarded myself with a sly grin as we made our way to camp and on through the gates of Ravensbrück.

"To the bath hall! Schnell, schnell, macht 'schnell!" came the cry from the head of the line. A strip-down search. My heart sank. We shuffled single file into the big cold hall that smelled faintly of mold and lye soap, and fairly reeked of unwashed bodies. I watched the other lines as mine moved forward slowly. Some women were completely unclothed; others were undergoing the most cursory of examinations. Please, God, that I should be so lucky. It was my turn. I stepped forward to bring my over-sized frame and smelly self as uncomfortably close to the guard as possible, and started an indignant rattling, looking her right in the eye.

"So you think I would have any of those dirty, lice-filled rags you have in Bekleidungswerk, fraulein? Ha! I don't have to steal that rot, that trash. You think I need silverware to eat the pig's slop you feed us? My mother sends me anything I want. I have lots of warm underwear..."

I talked and talked, trying to maintain eye contact to prevent her from doing a thorough search, or giving her a quiet moment to wonder about the over-sized, bulky work gloves I still wore. She looked in my hair, under my collar, patted my sides and ordered me past.

At the Warsaw Loot Place, we had two supervisors. One was a gentleman, kind and compassionate, who often told us, "If there is anything in my life that I regret, it is that I volunteered for the SS."

The devil in human form is the only fit description for the other supervisor—Mozeck. He had suffered three concussions, twice a cracked skull, and he had been in a mental institution for six months. Then they made him a supervisor in Ravensbrück, a women's concentration camp. The man obviously enjoyed beating women. He got sexual satisfaction from it. One woman with a shaved head asked him for permission to use a scrap of cloth to protect her bare, tender skin from the cold. He beat her, with no justification, until she could no longer stand, and all the while, he moaned and grunted, his breath coming faster and faster until she lay bloody and broken at his feet. His face gleamed behind a sheen of sweat.

Mozeck always yelled at us, and we shuddered at the first sound of his voice, the first echo of his polished boots on the wooden floors, but he could also be intimidated. He came into my work barracks carrying a whip made of five inch-wide strips of leather, with knots tied at each strip's end. He was walking hunched over and wild-eyed, what we called his hunter's look, and I knew I had to stop him before he got started. I grabbed the whip out of his hand, my eyes squinted, my voice hard. "Don't you come in here. I'm working with these women and they are efficient and fast. But when you come in, they get nervous and can't do anything."

"Give me my whip, drecksau."

"Yes, I will give you your whip, but first promise me that you won't beat any of them."

The look in his glazed eyes changed slightly, and he leered at me, his breath hot and stinking.

"I'll beat you, then."

He laughed a deep-throated gargle and my mouth went dry. I tapped the shaft of the whip on the palm of my other hand, and said with more strength than I really felt, "Go ahead, you can beat me to death, if you want. I'm not scared of you."

"You, why, you're hysterical," he sputtered.

"I know I'm hysterical," I almost shouted, my voice starting to break, "but I can tell you one thing. When I came to this camp, I wasn't hysterical, and if you want to report this to the Kommandant, I will tell him that you, Mozeck, you with your whip and your loud voice, have made me hysterical! Out! Out of here! Out of my sight!"

He went. He was actually frightened by my trumped-up rage. Once the door had shut on his hurried exit, I began to giggle nervously and the girls rushed over to comfort me so that my hysteria would not become a reality.

About an hour later, Mozeck returned to the depot, twisting the brim of his cap in his chubby fingers. "Don't get so excited, will you? I have much to think of, and I don't always realize what I say."

"You have much to think of?" I was incredulous. "Ha! I have much more to think of than you. When the Russians come, and they can come any day, then I have to worry about where I will be going. You have that whole bag of clothes that you have stolen from here for yourself and your little friend. You know how to escape from here. I don't."

It startled him that I knew so much about his thievery and his lover, one of the female guards. I should have known better than to reveal how much I had found out about his operations, but it seemed that the only way to survive the warped pleasures of the Nazis like Mozeck was to get your bluff in on them any way you could. Maybe I saved myself from a beating or two, but in the long run, it cost me much more.

The bread we ate was baked in Oranienburg-Sachsenhausen, a camp for men outside Berlin. It came in the same kind of freight cars that the Warsaw loot came in. One day, one of the girls discovered a car full of bread that should have gone on into the camp, instead of stopping at our depot. After examining the car, we found a barred opening on top. With blankets and pillows from the depot piled on top of each other, we made a little mountain of bedding to reach the opening and I climbed up on top, taking one loaf after another out through the open slats. The girls I worked with stood below, taking as much bread into their arms as they could.

"Mozeck!" We ran in all directions. I thought I could avoid him by running between the bread car and the one in front of it, but I bumped right into the monster as I cleared the other side. I had taken two loaves myself, tucking them into my jacket above the belt, so that now I looked like a freakishly heavy-breasted woman.

"What is it? What are you looking for?"

I was so taken aback that I could not think of a lie. "Bread. I was looking for bread. I am so hungry."

Mozeck was just as surprised as I was that the truth was on my lips, for instead of reacting in any expected manner, he just nodded and walked on past me. And there I was with my two loaves.

As the Russians approached from the east, all concentration camp prisoners were evacuated from Poland and eastern Germany, and most of the women came to Ravensbrück. We had neither room nor food enough for the women already there, so they built a gas chamber.

That's when the fitness inspections began. Anyone not productive and therefore a burden (the old, the chronically ill) were sent to the gas chamber. White haired women were doomed, no matter what their real age, and many of them put stove soot in their hair to try to fool the Nazis. On Sunday afternoons, we were marched round and round the camp in the heat of the day to the rhythm of the songs we sang until one by one, the women began dropping out from exhaustion. When the Nazis had a truckload, out they went through the camp gates, and the trucks soon came back—empty.

"We are sending you to a camp where the work will be easier for you," they told the women, "but first you must bathe." Most of them had to know what was coming, but perhaps they clung desperately to hope as the SS played out the charade to the bitter end, issuing a small bar of soap and a towel to each one. But only gas came out of the showerheads.

One Dutch prisoner I knew worked in the place where they kept all our personal belongings, and she told me a friend of hers had been notified she was to go on transport. The day after she was transferred, the first prisoner was sorting a stack of items that had just been brought in, when she came upon the shoes of her friend. "I recognized the shoes," she told me tearfully. "How can she be transferred without her shoes?"

I knew the fate of the women because a Dutchman from a nearby KZ had told me a gas chamber was being built. He was one of half a dozen who came by the depot every other day with a load of caskets headed for our crematorium. He was a ship builder from Wassenaar, a little place just outside The Hague, and one day he said that he would be seeing me a lot more often because with the new gas chamber and another oven, production would be up. One of my first impressions of the camp had been the smoke from the chimney of the crematorium, which was in sight above the camp's stone wall, and the smell of burned flesh. Sometimes when a new load was put in the ovens, a big flame leaped out, and on a still day, my mouth and nose were filled with the fetor of smoldering human bones.

I contracted pneumonia just before Christmas 1944 and though I tried to keep going, steeled myself to defeat the illness, I at last became too weak to get out of bed and I was taken to sickbay. During my lucid moments, I prayed to God that I would survive. I tried to picture myself at home in a beautiful church, surrounded by my family singing the familiar words of praise to God. I always enjoyed the liturgy of church and going to Mass is a treat, rather than an obligation. The ceremonies never became routine to me and the set order of Mass is reassuring, rather than boring. I was brought up in a home where religion was one of the most important facets of our daily lives. I took that for granted, though, never realizing it could be taken away from me. I was not a strong Christian then. We went to church because everybody went to church. But in Ravensbrück and the other prisons, I realized that the only strength I had, the only thing I could rely on, was my faith.

I knew that Christ had died on the cross for our sins, but I had always thought of it in terms of the great sins of the people in the whole world. I never stopped to think that he had died for me personally until I had nothing else in my life to think about. Christ's presence was so tangible; it was just as if every time I was beaten, someone held on to me, saying, "You can make it. You have strength and courage and I am here to help you." I felt it so clearly.

I had found a Polish woman, a Czech, a German and a French woman who all felt as strongly about their religion as I did. I never knew any religion but Catholicism because in Holland, the Catholics and Protestants were quite divided. I went to parochial school and didn't come into contact with friends of different religions, and I had never been inside another kind of church, except for the one time I attended the wedding of a friend in a synagogue. Mother was upset that I had entered the Jewish house of worship, but I saucily reminded her that Christ himself had done so regularly, and she had no answer for that. But the five of us, strong Catholics, walked together when we had time off and pretended to hold spirited conversations. In reality, we recited the prayers of Mass. We smiled at each other and gesticulated occasionally so that anyone watching us would not know we were breaking a strict rule. We were not material for martyrdom, none of us. We all wanted to survive.

Sickbay that winter was so overcrowded that other nearby barracks had been taken over to accommodate the hundreds of terribly ill or dying women. I had one under sheet, no covers, and we lay two women to a bed, three tiers high. The woman who shared my place of misery was French and suffered from dysentery. About every five minutes, she would have an attack, and sometimes she couldn't make it out of bed in time. The mess soaked the bed and splashed on me, and she was so ashamed. But there was nothing she could do to help herself. Each time, she cleaned the bed and ourselves as well as she could. She would have been beaten by the guard if she hadn't.

On Christmas Eve about nine o'clock, Claudine died. Just before she stopped breathing, she dirtied the whole bed. I was too weak to move; my cries for help went unheeded. Roll call and the alive/dead count had been taken for the day. Nothing would be done about one more dead body until the next roll call at seven a.m. on Christmas Day. My struggles to get up, my nausea from the putrid smell and my terror at spending the night with a corpse only added to my labored breathing and high fever. I prayed once more, but with a far more desperate plea: God, let me die. No more suffering. I've had enough. If you love me at all, please, I want to die.

I drifted in and out of consciousness during the long, lonely night, my fever rising and my mind filled with nightmares. Soldiers beat me, speeding trains crushed me and I suffered again through a frightening experience from my childhood. An unwanted guest had come to Grossvater's estate when I was five, and although he was not welcome in the castle, he was allowed to stay in one of a dozen small cottages where the servants lived. He had belonged to the Prussian nobility but had fallen to a low level through drinking, loose women and cards, my grandfather told me. Now he traveled from place to place, staying and eating for free until his host bought him a ticket to his next destination.

In the evening, the workers gathered outside the cottages to smoke their pipes, drink some beer and tell stories. Our guest joined them there, as I did, fascinated by their folklore and tales of tortured spirits. One evening as I walked alone back to the house, the man followed me into the trees and grabbed me, pulling at my clothes. I yelled as loud as I could and my brave little Heiko barked furiously, bringing the servants at a run. I was shaking all over when Grossvater picked me up, and kept me in bed for several days.

But now in my feverish state of mind, the fright continued, reality took over, and Grossvater never came.

At some point, my fever broke, and I lay awake and still, listening to the breathing of hundreds of women, holding myself away from the cooling body next to me. My wish to die was gone. I had remembered my brother and the Mass he said for me. I tried to conjure up my mother's face and that of my child. They were praying for me, I knew. I had to live to go home. One moment I had been eager to die, desperate for an easy way out. Now, I knew I would make it.

I was well enough to go back to my barracks on December 28. I still had a fever, but there were too many other women who needed my bed in sickbay. On New Year's Day 1945, I was listless and alone. I needed company. I made my way to Barracks 27, where the French women lived, seeking Ma Mere, the gentle Sister who had spent her life caring for foundlings until she made the mistake of taking in Jewish orphans.

When I entered the barracks, I was bombarded with the noise and confusion of hundreds of women talking at once, all in a gay mood because of the New Year and the hope of better things to come. It took me half an hour of wandering and asking directions to find Ma Mere's bunk. She was lying on bare bed slats because someone had stolen her sack of straw. I told her I would get it back for her, but she said, "No, Janette, perhaps it was someone who has a bad back. I can do without. I am comfortable."

We talked for a long time and she tried to bring me out of the depression I was feeling from being so sick and from thinking that there was never to be an end to our tribulations. She walked me to the door of the barracks when I said I had to leave, and took my hands, squeezing them gently. "France has forgotten the Lord, Janette. She has turned her back on the Lord, and maybe He wants a sacrifice from one of us, in order to save France. I would be so proud, so grateful, if I were the one who could make that sacrifice." It was the last time I looked upon her serene, love-filled face.

CHAPTER NINE

To Siberia and Prison Number 47

A dusting of clean, white snow covered the faces of the new corpses, and I brought my makeshift candle close as I brushed nature's pure cerement from each still face. It was not yet daybreak, but between the bitter cold that stabbed into my bones and the consuming ache of hunger that filled my awareness, I found it impossible to sleep through the night. In the early mornings, I wrapped my various garments around me and moved slowly among the stacks of frozen and freezing bodies outside my barracks and those buildings nearby, checking to see how many of the dead I knew. If I hadn't seen someone for a couple of days, it was more than likely they were dead, the victim of typhoid fever or another fast-moving disease, starvation or loss of hope.

Asocial or criminal women were assigned to picking up the corpses each morning as the rest of us walked wearily by the stacks on our way to our jobs. It was a horror to see. The pairs of women went all day long from one barracks to another, pulling a wooden cart behind them, a guard following at a distance. The bodies weren't just outside the buildings, but also lying naked in the washrooms within each block. If a woman died during the night, her bunkmates stripped off her clothing and took what possessions she might have, moving the still-warm body into the washroom. The corpse handlers, when they came at daylight, would each grab a leg of the nearest corpse and drag the body out to the cart. Then with one at her feet and one gripping her wrists, they swung the dead woman to and fro, then up, up onto the heap of meat and bones.

Sometimes at night, as the dark gathered and we came into camp "Te-ra-la-la, te-ra-la-la", singing as they bade us, we would meet that creaking wagon load of skin and leering faces, and we fell silent as we wondered how many of our companions had at last gained liberation that day.

There were more than 30,000 of us by the time winter came again, that last year in Ravensbrück. There was little we hadn't seen, eaten or been put through. I watched out a window one Sunday as a truck pulled up in front of the tuberculosis barrack. The weak, pale TB victims were pushed and shoved through the block door by the guards, the dying women clutching their flimsy undergarments that rippled in the icy wind. With much scrambling and boosting, the inmates were loaded onto the open truck bed, their bare feet slipping in the snow and mud until nearly all of them had fallen. One woman had come outside wrapped in a tattered blanket. A soldier shouted at her, struck her shoulder with the butt of his gun, then jerked the covering from her grasp. She was naked.

When the truck came back empty in about ten minutes, I knew their destination had been the gas chamber just outside camp. It was sickening, it was disheartening, but it was no longer shocking. Brutal death was commonplace, and some women looked on even the most painful endings as a blessed departure from hell. Besides, each death meant one less mouth to share the watery soup with; another garment or two to add to the warmth of whatever neighbor was quick enough to claim the spoils. One woman in the sickbay was still alive, yet in a coma, when another prisoner took the woman's slip, leaving her thin, emaciated body exposed to the drafts and chill of the night.

"She will no longer need it," the stronger woman reasoned to those of us who saw her, "and now I have two shifts."

Our lowest, basest instincts surfaced in Ravensbrück. I have been ashamed for a long time of my part in a similar incident. One of my friends in the block was dying. We dragged her to work with us, we held her upright between us at roll call, but we knew she couldn't last much longer. On a Sunday afternoon, our only time off, we sat around a table and our conversation was interrupted by the wailing of a siren.

"Come on, it's time for roll call," someone said to her as we pushed away from the table and headed outside, but she didn't move. Her shoulders were hunched, her head heavy upon her folded arms on top of the table. She had died right in our midst. She had been my friend. And my first reaction was to wonder if she had eaten all her ration. Hunger. Hunger makes you do things like that. All around me were signs that things were going to get worse—more terrible than I had ever dreamed possible, not just for the concentration camp, but for all of Germany. Food, which had been bad and scarce, became drier, more watery, thicker with mold, and delivered less often. It was harder to organize even the smallest item, because so much was being shipped to the Front or being stolen by the Nazis in and around camp. They were beginning to share our worries about where the next mouthful was coming from and how to keep the cold out.

When I was first taken prisoner, all my jewelry was confiscated, except my wedding ring. During that last winter, armed guards appeared suddenly in the door of our block and a supervisor demanded our gold bands. I couldn't get mine off, my hands were so swollen from the hard work and biting cold, so they cut the ring off. One woman there—Magdalena Dede—had the biggest, shouting, vulgar mouth that always dominated every conversation. We couldn't sit and talk to each other without her butting in and yelling obscenities if she disagreed. Somehow, she missed the hand inspection that day, and kept her ring. But a few days later, she made the mistake of talking back to a female guard, gesticulating with her hands.

"I see you still have your wedding ring, Dede," the guard commented quietly.

I have never seen a person's demeanor change as quickly as Frau Dede's did then. Her mouth closed, and her head dropped as she rubbed the smoothness of the band with her work-worn finger and thumb. It must have taken all her strength to raise that heavy head and look into the eyes of the waiting guard.

"Oh, no." It was more a pleading than a demand. "I've worn that ring for 50 years. You won't take that." But they did.

Two Jehovah's Witnesses refused to wear prison garb because they weren't criminals, and the SS left them outside in the snow, dressed only in pants and undershirt until they died. I saw a gypsy woman pull out her hair by the handfuls as she watched her small sons marched off to a truck and listened to their pitiful cries of

"Mama, mama." The cruelty, the apathy was frightening. It seems now that the SS could not possibly have been so inhuman, but they were.

The Russians were only 100 miles from Berlin in late January 1945: Several transports from the east brought more women each week. One Sunday I came back to my barracks to see a stranger talking to one of my block-mates. They were talking in Dutch and Flemish, which are very similar, and after the Belgian girl left, I struck up a conversation with the newcomer.

Thin as a stick, with big brown eyes and curly black hair, Ada was only 17. A Dutch Jew, she had been taken prisoner two years before, along with a brother and her parents. They had tried to escape from Holland to Switzerland by bribing a man with 1000 guilders, but he sold them out to the Gestapo. The family was arrested at the railroad depot and sent to Auschwitz, where Ada's father and brother were gassed. Her mother died of typhoid just before evacuation began.

From Auschwitz, the prisoners walked westward for three days and nights. Anyone who couldn't keep up was shot. Open freight cars brought them to Ravensbrück, and we were all confined to barracks while the new arrivals disembarked. They had suffered badly from the sub-zero temperatures and the smell of rotting fingers, noses and ears permeated the camp. Ada had been immediately taken to sickbay for treatment of scarlet fever and had just been released when I met her.

It was good to have someone to talk Dutch to and we developed an almost instant rapport, talking through the afternoon and on into the evening. She told me her life story, which she said she had never repeated to anyone. I felt as if I should take her under my wing, she was still such a child, and we met every day after work. One day, the Kommandant, doctor and work division leader called all of us out and ordered us to take our shoes and socks off, then march past them so they could look for swollen legs. The ones with bad legs were taken out and told they were going on transport.

When I got back to the barracks, someone told me, "There has been a girl here, a girl with brown eyes and black hair, and she asks you to come to Barracks 28."

Barracks 28. Poor Ada. The gas chamber anteroom. Enclosed by chicken wire, the big barracks held all women "on transport" until they could be processed. I went at once. She stood in the enclosure, her hands gripping the thin wire, her eyes huge, her face blanched.

"They tell us we are going on transport, Johanna, they say we are being transferred, but I have been in Auschwitz. I know what this means. This is gas."

"I am only 17." She began to cry. "I don't want to die."

I promised to get her out. I didn't know at all how I could do it, but she needed reassurance, and I had to try my best. That evening, I talked to nearly everyone I knew, even a woman who was in Work Division, seeking help, but there was no one willing or able to save Ada. I was desperate. My mind could not rest. I got no sleep. But still, the next morning, a solution eluded me.

We gathered for roll call, standing first as separate barracks and then in formation for work details. An idea came to me suddenly. Would it work?

I ran to Barracks 28. Ada waited for me in the gray dawn, not hopeful, knowing she was doomed, but still showing that she trusted and believed in me. The guard, an older man, paced back and forth in front of the barracks gate, rifle on his shoulder. I came to stiff attention before him. "I would like to get Prisoner Number 104852 out of here."

The old man stopped in his tracks, raising an eyebrow incredulously. "Nobody comes out of here," he said emphatically and moved to continue his pacing.

"Wait a moment," my voice was trembling, unsure. I licked my lips and cleared my throat. "She is the best worker I have in Bekleidungswerk 1, and you know how important that is for the war, that we work as quickly as possible."

He pursed his lips, thinking, unsure of what to do, but unable to leave his post to ask someone else.

"She will have to be back here tonight," he ventured.

"Of course! Where else?"

"Then she can go."

I turned to a disbelieving Ada. "Come on, you. Out of there. Come on! Schnell! Schnell!"

She had never worked with me and she was in no condition to work anywhere, so I told her only to sit, unless a guard came in. That evening, I took her back to her purgatory. The next morning, I gained her release again and she returned at dark. But each morning she reported another 25-30 women had been taken while she was gone. I had to think fast.

The head of Work Division, Flomm, was at Barracks 28 the fourth morning I went after Ada. He was a friend of Mozeck, the evil supervisor. I had most recently seen him in my work place, where he had come to pick up silk for handmade shirts—an illegal gift from Mozeck.

I stood at attention. "I am 20442, Johanna, come to pick up 104852, VanEsso, Ada."

He looked me up and down, sneering. "Nobody comes out of here. You know that."

"But, sir, I beg to bring it to your attention that VanEsso is the only one who knows anything about different materials. She works with me in Bekleidungswerk 1. You remember last week, when you got that silk for your shirts?"

I saw fear spring into his eyes. "Why is she in this barracks?"

"I don't know. It must be a mistake, because she is the healthiest, hardest working help I have."

"Then she should be in your barracks," he smiled tightly. "You must talk to this blockova and then to your own."

I thanked him and clicked my heels together, requesting permission to leave. I ordered Ada from the compound, telling her, as we walked away. "Don't show a thing. Walk straight. Don't look back." I could feel the eyes of Flomm and the guard boring into my back. Once we turned a corner and were out of their sight, Ada grabbed me and hugged me tight. "Thank God I'm out of there. There were so few left when I came in last night."

A few days later, the supervisor of all the work divisions, Opitz, an officer who came by rarely, entered the depot and found a package of material. As I said, no one was allowed to take things from there except by requisition, and an older woman was employed all day documenting the yards and colors of cloth goods. Opitz knew there was no legitimate reason for the material to be wrapped up.

"What is in that package?" Opitz asked me, since I was unit leader, but I said I didn't know. "You never know anything, swine. What good are you?"

He tore back the wrapping and exposed several yards of fine silk. Turning furiously upon the measuring woman, he shouted, "You put that aside, eh? You were going to take the silk to your fine home?" He raised his hand to strike her.

"No!" He stopped at my shout. "I beg your pardon, Herr Obersturmführer Opitz. I remember now who the package belongs to. It was Miss Nellie's. She put that aside, just like last week when she got your permission to do that."

Miss Nellie was a guard, but she was also mistress to Mozeck, a married man with six children. She always whined, "Leo, can't I have that? It is so beautiful, and no one will miss such a small thing." And he always gave in.

"My permission?" stormed Opitz. "I gave no one permission for such thievery. Go and get this Miss Nellie!"

I ran to the office and asked for Nellie, but the guard on duty told me Nellie was sick and only came in to work in the afternoon. I repeated that to Opitz.

"What kind of pig sty is this? Where is Mozeck? Go and get Mozeck. Now!"

Opitz gave him quite a dressing down. He thundered in Mozeck's face, "When I say you are a bit of shit, then you are a bit of shit!"

"Ja wohl," Mozeck cried, and clicked his heels together. "Ja wohl." It was the way a soldier had to respond to an officer, no matter what his superior might be saying.

We workers had hidden behind a huge pile of yard goods, choking on our laughter at such a delightful incident. But then Opitz left, and Mozeck turned on us.

"Who told Obersturmführer Opitz that Miss Nellie had put the material aside?" We could barely hear him, he spoke so quietly.

"It was me."

"You! And why did you do that?"

"Because he would have beaten Frau Fuchs for stealing."

"And so what?"

"Aren't you ashamed? She is old enough to be your mother."

I had gone too far. "You dare to compare that dirty swine with my mother," he screamed. Mozeck threw me to the floor, beating and kicking me. There was no one courageous enough, nor strong enough to stop him. He nearly killed me.

That evening, as we made our way back to camp, I knew I must never go back to the depot. Each dragging footstep was matched by a prayer on my tongue. Strengthen me, Lord. Liberation can be only a matter of days away. Don't let me die now. Keep Mozeck away from me.

I talked to a girl in Work Division that night, telling her that I knew Mozeck would be just biding his time until he could finish what he had started. There was no one to stop him from murdering me. She knew, as did everyone in camp, what a maniac Mozeck was, and that I was in terrible danger. She said she would see what could be done, and two days later, both Ada and I had new work assignments. We never set foot again in the Warsaw Loot Place.

It was on a Thursday that I was beaten. A two-hour march on Saturday brought us to a big estate belonging to Obergruppenführer Pohl, who was Himmler's right hand. About 90 prisoners worked the fields and lived in one barracks, including Poles, Jehovah's Witnesses and about 15 Dutch women. Ada and I thought we had died and gone to heaven. If I would have had to live there for the rest of my life, I wouldn't have objected, because compared to camp, it was heaven. Each of us had our own bed, no more five women to two beds. Nobody had lice. I got a hot shower when I came, which I hadn't had for three years. Clean clothes, clean underwear and an apron were issued by the Dutch blockova.

There was such camaraderie among the prisoners, it was marvelous. Unlike in the camp, where you could trust no one, the change of atmosphere had us all talking together like old friends, singing and telling jokes. The next day, Sunday, we didn't work at all, except that we four new ones had to peel potatoes. Monday and Tuesday, we worked in the fields, but on Wednesday, we returned to Ravensbrück. The Russians had come, at last.

A car picked up the four of us who had just arrived that morning. When are the others coming? Are they behind us? How is it that we deserve such luxury? My questions went unanswered. Back at the camp, I was singled out and locked in the bunker, joining two Czech women already in one of the cells. They told me that some of their country women had told the Russians they were anti-Communist and the soldiers immediately put them in jail. "How about you?"

"I have often voiced my opinions about the Russians and Communism. I am a Catholic and I cannot condone their ways."

"We are all three in the same boat, then," one of them muttered.

We fell silent. I refused to believe it. Not after all this time, not after having waited an eternity for the Russians to save me. This cannot be happening to me. But it was. The three of us spent about a week in that dirty, dank cell. We had good food to eat, much better than the Germans had provided. The guard even brought a mattress at night and blankets. The Russians were not abusive in any way, but we were more frightened by their lack of action. What would become of us?

The door opened and a guard prodded us out to a truck. At last, something. Perhaps today our trials will be held, and we will have a chance to find out what charges are being made and what we can do about them.

Closed cattle cars hauled us eastward at the pace of a snail. Troop transports and car after car of wounded soldiers took precedence over a motley group like us, and our small train spent days at a time sitting idle on sidetracks. We three scarecrows and a trainload of Nazi big shots were on our way to Russia. No trial. No charges. With each turn of the metal wheels, I was going further away from my son.

The high society Nazis looked down their noses at us, as if it were our fault that we were in such miserable shape, and tried to keep away from us. But we were packed like so many little fish in a tin can, and it wasn't long before they neither smelled nor looked any better than we did. There was no toilet of any kind and the guards would not let us get out during our frequent stops. The straw on the floor was changed every other day, but the lice, which we had brought with us from the bunker, remained and multiplied. Sometimes when the guards opened the doors, we could see beautiful farmland stretching out for miles, but we had no idea where we were, nor what our destination was.

The food wasn't too bad. They regularly gave us thick soup, bread and water, but we were all exhausted because we couldn't all sit at the same time, there were too many bodies, and we had to take turns. Then even when my legs ached with relief at getting the weight off them, my lungs heaved and choked and I wondered how long I could continue to breathe the putrid close air at the bottom of the car. The only openings, other than the crack of the door, were at the very top of the car, feet above even my tall head.

The time was interminable. Day and night blended together, and we spent increasingly longer periods of time motionless. The air inside the cattle cars was rank and heavy, and people became nauseated and were sick, which only added to the smell. The guards made sure our living quarters were mucked out at least every other day, and they changed their minds on letting us out for fresh air. Maybe they thought we were far enough into Russia that it would do no good for someone to try to escape. We milled around outside our respective cars as they used buckets of cold water to rinse off some of the filth on the floor. Everyone tried to use these intervals to take care of their toilet needs, but even then there was no privacy. The last time they opened the doors on that terrible trip, I found out later we had been on the tracks for six weeks, there was a sign evidently indicating a town ahead, but neither my Czech companions nor I could decipher it. Although Czech and Russian sound a lot alike, they use different alphabets.

Big transports, like buses with no seats or windows, took us to a prison within a small town. A hole in the roof of the bus allowed some fresh air in and our ears began to absorb the unfamiliar sounds of people calling out greetings, bells ringing on passing bicycles, motor noises. We were put in one big room that disclosed unexpected luxuries, two separate bathrooms. We asked for washcloths, they gave us a few, and one after the other, we reached the little sinks in the toilet cubicles, scrubbing hurriedly at our scummy hides. When you're as dirty as that, you don't even give a community wash cloth a second thought. I was in heaven at the touch of cold water against my dirt-caked, scaling skin.

We stayed in that first room for about a week. Every day, people were taken out for interrogation, big shot Nazis first; some came back and some didn't. Even though we sometimes heard what sounded like gunshots outside, I don't know that those people were executed. We speculated then that the prisoners were being transferred in small groups. No sooner would 10-15 people be taken out than 20-25 new prisoners arrived in their places. There weren't just Germans, but all nationalities, even a few Russians. As in all the other prisons, I found myself constantly guarding my tongue, never knowing whether the prisoner complaining bitterly next to you was really suffering, or if he was a Russian spy or troublemaker.

The three of us still kept together—Anuschka, Maria and I— and tried to stay out of the frequent quarrels that sprang up between the Nazis. Even though they were captives of the Russians, and the Third Reich a failure, the prominent Nazis felt all the other prisoners should pay homage to them. We were all on the same helpless level, but they continued to look upon us as a sub-human species, abusing our few rights as often and as much as they dared. We took less and less of their reviling, as we began to get our strength and confidence back. After all, we were no longer in Nazi Germany. Our fears were projected towards the Russians and what lay in store for us.

It surprised me, and perhaps it was a reflection of what went wrong with Hitler's dream, but the Nazis refused to hold together and help each other. They quarreled constantly. Several knuckled under to the derisive select few, thinking, I suppose that there was some small chance they might soon be back in Nazi Germany, and they should cover all their bases, just in case. The social stratification of the Party was so ingrained, they could not believe that it had all ended, that they were free to, at least, think for themselves again.

A basic difference between captivity under the Nazis and the same situation under Russian authority, and an important variation, was that the Russian guards were indifferent to their charges. We were neither racial threats, political enemies nor objects of satiation to them. They brought our food; they took prisoners out and brought more in; they never talked, they never abused us. Like zombies, the men never expressed any emotion.

My Czech friends and I were shipped out in a large group of prisoners in about a month. My heart skipped a beat as I thought of what "transport" had meant to us at Ravensbrück, and my mind echoed once again with the question of where Ada was. Had she been liberated or did she lie among the skeletons of Ravensbrück? Be with Ada, dear Lord, as you are with me. Keep her from harm and give her the courage to make a life for herself. Here I am again, with no friend in the world but You. My life is in Your hands. We've made it this far together, and my trust is in You alone. I pray that You will be beside me as I face this new challenge.

The Russian guards marched us right down the main street of town, from the prison to the railroad, and the townspeople acted as if we weren't there. They paid no attention at all, even less than they might have to a herd of cattle, and I wondered if it was from fear of the soldiers, or just a lack of interest in anything outside their own survival.

We rode in passenger cars this time, as we once again headed eastward, with only hard wooden benches to sit on and no heat, but at least they weren't cattle wagons. It was mid-July and the heat during the day was almost unbearable, but at night we shivered and huddled together to keep warm. The only blessing about the ice-cold darkness was that it kept the swarms of mosquitoes away. Our faces, necks and arms had turned into swollen blotches.

We were moved six times between the first prison and our final destination: Prison No. 47. Each new jail was in a smaller town, successively closer to interior Russia. The further east, we traveled the filthier the cages, the coarser the food, the more ignorant the guards. In one of the aging, crumbling strongholds, the warden stayed drunk all the time, staggering and stumbling about, raging at us in a language we did not understand. Mostly, the guards used motions to instruct us. When we arrived at the final prison, we didn't know for a long time that it was to be permanent, for there was no one to tell us so.

Prison No. 47 lay between the two large cities of Omsk and Tomsk, I found out later, deep within Russia. I think, from its appearance that it had once been a school, or perhaps a military barracks. Female employees came from outside the prison to do the office work, but there were no female guards. Prisoners did the cooking and cleaning. Everyone wanted kitchen duty, of course, but I was not so lucky. The two-story brick building was in the shape of a "u", with a square of green grass in the center, and no surrounding wall. On one side, all women: the other side, all men: and in the bottom of the "u", families. The idea was preposterous to me at first, but it was eventually explained to me that Russians convicted of a small crime and sentenced to six months or so were allowed to have their wives and children live with them, as long as they paid for their own upkeep. The man went to work in the morning, albeit of a different sort of labor, and at night his wife had dinner waiting for him. I had nothing to do with these families, as we weren't allowed to go from one wing of the prison to another, but I could talk to some of the inmates as we worked side by side. I still understood very little Russian, but the Czech women with me could make out quite a bit of what was said, and they translated for me until we were separated. No one there spoke Dutch or English, but some knew German or French.

Women were in the minority in this prison, so for the first time in years, I had my own bed and the semblance of privacy. We had no mattresses on our double-tiered beds, but slept on sacks of straw without sheets, although they were overly generous with blankets. It was late summer when I arrived there, so we had no use for the blankets, but the Russian prisoners warned us not to tell the guards we didn't need the blankets because they would take them away and never give them back, even for winter. We stowed the bulky covers in storage cupboards that lined a big room we all slept in. The Russians were stingy with clean clothing. It had to be requisitioned from the supply room and the supply clerk always tried to talk the inmates out of whatever they thought they needed. Our camp was on the very fringe of Siberia, and the hot summers were short. Often, we stood waiting in the morning until the men could clear a path through three to four feet of snow. Once we were deep into winter, the surplus blankets proved to be more weight than warmth, and the women often slept two in a bed in an effort to keep warm. The only special clothing issue we got for the cold season was a pair of work mittens, just to keep our fingers from freezing and thus hindering our production ability.

I wouldn't have thought food could be prepared to taste any worse than what we had been reduced to at Ravensbrück, but the Russians managed to do just that. We got a coarse gruel in the morning that sometimes boasted a few pieces of stringy fish and a hunk of bread, which I saved to keep me going during the long day. In late evening, we stood in line again for our ration of a thick soup called borscht, and then we always got a cup of tea, and once in a while a bit of sugar. At times, we were treated with sugar once a week, then maybe not again for two weeks, or perhaps every four days. The Russians were nothing like the systematic Germans. I still ask myself how they could have known how many prisoners they had; their accounting for everything was so erratic. We never registered, were not assigned numbers. No one interrogated me or asked my name, age or why I was a prisoner. There must have been 150 people gathered in the prison yard when our group arrived, and we stood through an extensive, incomprehensible speech by the camp commandant, but there was no checkpoint afterward to match prisoners with papers, if the Russians even had any identification for us.

At first there were not many criminals in the women's section, but more and more were brought in, and things went steadily down hill. First, they took over the food rationing and our chunks of bread got smaller, the liquid in our bowls shallower. It did no good to complain to the guards. They drank heavily and held no sympathy for us, and the racketeers got even with complainers.

There wasn't much that went on there that everybody in the prison didn't know about. We weren't allowed to go into the other wings, but still, somehow, the information filtered back and forth and we learned a little bit about everyone who lived there. A huge giant of a man was in for murder, I found out, and I couldn't help but stare at him when I passed him outside. A chain was welded around his ankle, and he had to drag a big ball that was on the end of that chain, like they used to do to the slaves. He looked so mild and gentle, I thought, but he had found his wife in bed with another man and had killed them both.

Not only were we not registered when arriving at the prison, but also there was no search, either, so that sometimes a criminal could get in with a knife or other weapon. One woman had a short, razor-edged knife that she terrorized us with for many weeks. We did whatever she ordered us to do, for fear she might slit our throats in the middle of the night. She slept with the knife under her pillow, but one night several of the other criminal women joined together and beat the woman unconscious, taking her knife away from her. But then the leader of that group had a weapon, and we weren't that much better off. I don't know where the knife finally disappeared to, but I was grateful that it was gone.

While the Germans had felt themselves to be too far above us to mingle, the Russians were just the opposite. But at least they didn't force themselves on us. There were several women, especially among the criminal section, who would disappear in the evening and not come back until early in the morning. The guards offered bribes of sugar or vodka and I couldn't condemn the women for trying to better their circumstances, though I don't know where they found the energy or strength to stay up half the night, then work all day as hard as I did.

Deep basins below the latrines acted as reservoirs to hold what came from the toilets. With a bucket and wheelbarrow, I transported the contents from there to a larger basin. After I had emptied the wheelbarrow, a second worker filled it with sand and I took that load to a second place, dumped that, got a load of fine gravel, and returned to the latrines to repeat the process. I gave up saving my breakfast bread to eat during the day, because I did not want to touch the food with my hands while I was working, and my appetite was fairly quelled by the stench, so I didn't suffer too much hunger during the day. But, at night, as I lay in my filth, I cried from hunger and exhaustion and loneliness. I determined that I would leave this place and go home, at last, to Holland.

CHAPTER TEN

Escape from Siberia

Cakes were baked and brought in by women from the surrounding farming community that Christmas of 1945, the first Christmas treat I had enjoyed in five years. Living on a diet of porridge, coarse ground bread and salty, stringy fish, I would have welcomed any change. I could hear the voices of the men in their quarters, joined together in melancholy song, and I longed for home.

Up in the morning at four, I was never fully rested after the previous day's hard work before I had to begin another. In the evening, there was no set time that we had to be in bed, as there was in Germany, but I sought my pallet soon after returning to the dormitory, if not to sleep, at least to lie quietly and give free-rein to my thoughts. There was only one woman whom I really liked there, Olga, a former university professor from Moscow. She spoke French beautifully and we spent hours discussing French literature and the places she had traveled to. A sophisticated woman, Olga had acted as envoy for Russia until the government officials had discovered that her exposure to Western culture and politics had liberated her too much for their liking. Olga had become less than a devoted Communist, voiced a few unpopular opinions, and they had locked her up in this isolated prison.

Life dragged on until I thought in terms of how many buckets equaled a day, how many slices of bread equaled a week, how many freezing mornings and searing days equaled a season. I still thought of home and my family, but the memories had faded and the hope that I could ever leave Russia was nearly gone. It was just a few days before Christmas 1948 as we lined up to march to work when I turned to look at one of the guards just as he crossed himself, in the manner of the Russian Orthodox.

His name was Piotr, and he had been at the prison only a few short months. His manner was gentle and kind, and I knew that he spoke German, that he had been in Germany in 1945 with the first troops. So I began that day to seek his friendship, at first, only a comment or two about the weather or some work problem. He seldom acknowledged that I had spoken, but I knew he heard me, and that he was suspicious of my motives. Sometimes he answered; sometimes he only nodded, then turned away from me. But he didn't stop me, didn't order me to be silent, as another guard might have. It was like courting a bashful reluctant beau, except that I had more serious business in mind. He was too shy and hesitant to talk at any length. It took me a year and a half to reach the point where he trusted me enough to respond and carry on a conversation.

Once I finally got his ear, I rattled off as much about the past ten years—this was January 1950—that I could condense into a quarter of an hour. I told him that I had been incarcerated in Ravensbrück and re-imprisoned in Russia only for my political views, that I was not a criminal, and had received no trial prior to my banishment to this Siberian outpost. "My son, if he is still alive, will be nine in May, Piotr, and I saw him only on the day of his birth. If my mother is still alive, I am sure he is in good care, but I long to be with him, to know him, to touch him."

At first, his face registered only skepticism, but the longer I talked, describing my husband and his death, the work we had done for the underground, the way I had been trapped into signing the Schutzhaft-papers, the less Piotr doubted me. Once I felt that he sympathized with me, I quietly broached the subject of needing his help to escape. But he wanted nothing to do with such a plan. It was impossible, he said abruptly, and I felt a stab of disappointment. But I was too determined to let that stop me. I asked him not to tell anybody that I had asked and he agreed not to, if I would forget about escaping. This went on for two weeks.

"Piotr, I cannot forget about it," I announced. "How can a mother forget about her child, who is a part of herself? I know you love children. I have seen you with the children here. I've watched you from my upstairs window, and you never pass through the courtyard without stopping to talk with them, or to pat one on the head. Do you have a child of your own?" Instant pain winged across his features and we were both silent for a few minutes. What had I said? Had I perhaps just destroyed the relationship it had taken me two years to build?

"I had a child," Piotr said finally. "It was born dead, and my wife died shortly afterward."

I covered his hand with mine and looked into his grieving eyes. "But my child, Piotr, is not dead, or at least he wasn't when I was taken away. I gave birth to him and he was healthy and beautiful, but my mother is old and cannot care for him indefinitely. What will happen to my Frans if my mother dies and he is alone in Holland, his mother far away in a Russian prison?"

I silently prayed for Piotr's forgiveness and Christ's indulgence for the way I was using the young soldier. I did not lie to him, but I did neglect to tell him that I had four brothers and three sisters who would have taken care of Frans if it became necessary. I had to play on his sympathy, work on his sense of justice, and use his friendship to gain my freedom. "You know what it will cost me if I am caught?" His question, I knew was leading to a commitment. "I will be here for the rest of my life, not as a guard, but as a prisoner. That is, if I am not executed on the spot."

There was nothing I could say in reply. I just sat there, waiting for him to finish reasoning it out for himself. It took only a few minutes before he had an escape plan. The peasants who farmed the area around the prison supplemented their meager incomes by selling the hides of wild animals to the prison, which in turn took the hides to the nearest village and sold them there. The guards took turns driving the wagon that hauled the collected skins away, one day to town, one day to trade the hides, then one day back to the prison. Piotr didn't know when he would be ordered to take his turn, but when he did, I could go with him.

I think every waking moment from that time on must have been spent in prayer by both of us—Piotr praying he would not get caught and I, begging for the day to come soon. I also spent the interval scrounging for things I would need, and came up with a stubby, half-dull knife, two boxes of matches, a ball of string and a cross. Years before, one of the girls who had been interned there for only a short time had made a little cross from two pieces of root nailed together and she had given it to me before she left.

Piotr had sent word at last, and I stood in the courtyard, trying to mingle with the other women, failing to think of the most casual comment, my palms dripping with sweat. At last I was able to slip away, darting behind a building and practically slithering over to the hide wagon and in under a pile of stiff, hairy covers that nearly suffocated me with their perfume of rancid tallow and decaying meat. Piotr had to get all the hides loaded, regardless of the room I took up, so by the time he was finished, I was nearly groaning from the pressure on top of me, but I would have cut my own tongue out before I made a sound.

The sound of voices was muffled by the hides, but my heart stood still at the first noise. What were they saying? I could not make out the words, but the tone sounded questioning. Were they suspicious? Was someone about to jam a manure fork into the skins to prompt a confession of my presence? Dear Lord, don't let me sneeze. I tried to control my breathing to a low, unmoving rate, for fear that the slight raising and lowering of my chest might be detected. The back of my throat began to tickle. I could not cough, nor make the slightest clearing sound. I swallowed hard, trying to ease the irritation. Think of something else. Think of home, of Frans, Mother, of Holland. Next month will be nine years exactly since I saw any of them.

The voices rose in farewell, I was sure of it, and then the cart started moving. Thank you, God; thank you, Piotr, thank you, guards, for letting us go. Soon the movement of the cart and the heat of the morning sun through the hides lulled me to sleep, and my last thought was that I would just rest a moment until Piotr stopped and let me get up on the seat beside him.

I was soaked in sweat, scummy with dust and hair, and nearly dying of thirst when I awoke. How long had it been since we left the prison? Why hadn't Piotr stopped? Surely, we must be far enough away by now. I cannot spend the entire day beneath this terrible weight. I pushed upwards on the hides above me, then stopped suddenly. What if there was someone with Piotr, riding beside him, there to witness my arrival if I came crawling out of the stinking cargo? Perhaps that was why he hadn't stopped before. Have patience, Johanna; don't ruin everything by succumbing to a little weakness. But still, I lay there, straining to hear voices, but only the steady beat of the horse's hooves on the road came through.

At last, the wagon stopped and Piotr began peeling back hides to help me out. He was alone, and I had nearly suffocated from his abundance of caution, but I couldn't blame him. After all, he was taking a great risk for me.

"I was afraid to look back to see if we were alone on the road, Johanna," he explained apologetically. "I thought if someone saw me turn around, they would be suspicious and follow us. I had to act as if everything were normal."

Still, he didn't let me sit with him in the front of the cart. "It's too dangerous, do you understand? There may be someone in the woods or in the fields whom we can't see, yet they can see us, and will report us." So I lay flat in the center of the hides, out in the air, at least, and Piotr kept a sharp eye for any travelers or farmers. When someone was first sighted, he would warn me and I would creep under the hides again.

When it was almost evening, Piotr pulled on the reins and spoke to the horse. He turned in his seat and told me, "I want to let you out here, not too close to the village. I don't want anybody to see us, and these woods will keep you out of sight for quite a long way."

With that, he gave me a loaf of bread and two onions, which had been packed for him. I put the food, my knife, cross and ball of string into my scarf and tied it into a bundle. We had already decided I must travel northwesterly to Finland. Poland was occupied by the Communists, as was part of Germany, we knew from new prisoners at No. 47, so Finland was the closest free country where I could hope for asylum.

"I tried to get you a compass," Piotr said, "but I just couldn't do so without arousing suspicion. Stay in the woods. Don't trust anyone too far..." We smiled at each other as he repeated all the things we had gone over time and time again during the past few weeks.

I stepped into the trees and waited until Piotr and the cart were out of sight. The clip-clop of the horse, the creaking wheels had gone too. The only sound was my own heartbeat steady in my ears, my shirtsleeve against a bush, the sigh of mud as I picked up my foot and took my first step in the direction Piotr had indicated. I was a woman alone in the heart of Russia, walking toward a country that might deny me entry, armed only with a dull, rusty knife and an undying faith in God.

Every morning, I awoke to the sun's first rays, and charted my course away from the rising light. I disciplined myself to eat as little of the bread and onions as possible, though I had the urge to eat the whole loaf at once, and supplemented my diet with berries and roots that were tender and filling. It was early spring, and the ground had yet to thaw in some parts of the forest, the nights staying cold, but I had matches, and the childhood training in climbing trees, jumping creeks with a pole, making and using a bow and arrows. I praised Grossvater daily for making me a "guy" and giving me the knowledge that was saving my life. I shot birds and rabbits with my crude arrows, skinning and gutting them with my little knife, and when those delicacies were elusive or unavailable, I turned to other small animals, like squirrels. Squirrel meat is awfully tough, no matter how long you roast it over a campfire. It would have been better, perhaps, had I boiled it, but I had no pot to cook with. After the bread and onions had been eaten, and when the berries had fallen from the bushes, I subsisted on a diet of pure protein.

I was surprised at how gentle the animals and birds in the forest were, but I suppose they didn't know that they should fear me, being unfamiliar with humans. I walked through places that might never have been entered by men, because I was afraid to get too close to civilization, for fear the good people would turn me in to the police. I never heard shots or voices or even the sound of domestic animals while I was in those woods. I've been told it is unsportsmanlike to shoot a bird that's sitting down, but I had no qualms about it at the time. The curious, unmoving partridges fell before my bow, and I was grateful for their presence and tender, life-sustaining flesh.

There was only one night in the first three weeks of walking that I was frightened at night. I heard movement in the bushes around the little clearing I had chosen to camp in, and beyond the light of my fire, I saw the glint of several pairs of eyes. I knew that Siberia has wolves and that the only thing that frightened them was fire, so I stayed awake all night, adding sticks of wood to my campfire every few minutes, my tired eyes moving from side to side in anticipation of the sudden rush of a 200-pound, murderous beast.

Because of the terrain, it wasn't always possible for me to go in a straight line to the northwest, but I tried to maintain that direction as I plowed through the forest for five-and-a-half weeks. I counted the days—38—and when I saw that the woods were about to end, I cautioned myself, aloud, as I had become in the habit of doing. I went from one extreme to another, convincing myself that there was a policeman waiting behind the next bush, or, on the other hand, reasoning that they probably hadn't even missed me at the prison.

My first day in the open, I felt unprotected, as if a thousand eyes were trained upon me, but I saw no one, found no sign of civilization. It is an odd sensation to wonder if perhaps something has happened and you might be the only person left in the world. But the next day, I saw a house in the distance. I hesitated. What am I to do? I have no food, and I have not eaten in two days. There are no berries or roots in this grassland, no animals and few birds. I had discarded my bow and arrows since I knew I wouldn't have any targets and they were just an added burden. What kind of people might live in this house? It can't be too far back to the prison. They will know I have escaped from there, and they will bind me up and carry me off to the nearest village. Come now, Johanna. The Lord has brought you this far; surely he will continue a few steps more so that you can get something to eat.

There was no one at work in the fields around the house. Perhaps this is an abandoned farm, I thought, and there will be nothing to eat here. But a woman opened the door at my knock, and stared open-mouthed at this creature that darkened her doorstep. I must have been quite a sight, spending all that time in the woods with nothing to cleanse myself with, no brush for my hair.

I raised my little cross and her eyes fastened on it. I repeated the Russian word for "food" a number of times, and made eating-like gestures. Her eyes moved from the cross to my hand, following it to my mouth, then all the way down my disheveled frame. She asked me a question, but I shook my head. I didn't understand. She motioned with her head, as if to say, "Come in", then stepped back into the room, opening the door wider. A twinge of fear ran through me and I almost bolted and ran, but I knew this was my only chance of survival on the plains. I had to trust the farmers.

An old man sat next to the kitchen fireplace, and the woman spoke questioningly to him, as if she needed him to reaffirm her decision to allow me in the house. I looked upon his wrinkled, compassionate face, and nearly cried out, "Grossvater!" He reminded me so much of my grandfather. I smiled and held up my little cross to him, and he nodded and said, "Da, da", which is "yes" in Russian, then spoke to the woman.

She went at once to her cupboard and brought out pots and pans, filling them with food, and shoving the kettles into the coals of the fireplace. I ate then, as I hadn't in so long. What she gave me was not a big dinner, just some meat dishes and vegetables that had evidently been cooked for their last meal, but it was regular, normal food, not roots and berries, or half-raw squirrel. When I was finished, I said, "I am tired, I want to sleep", laying the side of my head against my clasped hands. The old man and the woman spoke again to each other, then he motioned me to a pallet above and to the side of the fireplace. I slept at once, waking only hours later when another man, the woman's husband, entered the hut.

The old man—either her father or her husband's father, I thought—talked very excitedly, pointing towards the place where I slept. I could see them from my darkened resting spot, and I knew the newcomer didn't like the idea of having me there, but the old gentleman eventually convinced him that it was all right. In Russia, the people have much respect for their elders.

I drifted back to sleep, waking to find that the woman had prepared an omelet for my breakfast. The last time I had eaten an omelet had been in 1939. I hadn't tasted an egg since the Nazi bribed me with two for an Oriental rug. When I had finished, she gave me a slab of buttered bread, a wedge of cheese and a big slice of ham, which I carried away in my scarf. Her generosity brought tears to my eyes, and I thanked her over and over, bowing and smiling, as I set off once more. The old man stood outside the door, and pointed in a direction that was not northwest, as if indicating that I should head that way if I wanted to be safe. I thanked him and walked as he indicated, but it was straight north, and I angled off to the west as soon as I was out of his sight. It was another full day before I came to a house again.

It never failed that when I came to a peasant's home and showed my little cross, they welcomed me, fed me and provided me with a soft place to rest. I never entered a town, nor did I stop at every house I came to, but made a detour whenever I was faced with any sizeable gathering of civilization. Sometimes, the women gave me a piece of clothing when they saw the state of disrepair my belongings were in, often a babushka to protect my head from the summer sun. The only gift of clothing I needed and never got was a pair of shoes. I had worn shoes in the prison, but it didn't take long before the mileage destroyed them, and I had to rely on rabbit skins or scarfs to bind my feet and protect them from the rocks, thorns and hot ground I encountered. That's why I almost always needed the babushka that was offered—not for my head, but for my feet.

I spent a week with an old woman who lived alone. There were people working in the fields, but none of them lived with her. I noticed a picture of a man in a uniform and she pointed at it, saying, "Moscow". I think it was her son. Just before I left her gracious hospitality, she beckoned me into her sleeping room, dug through a pile of clothing on top of a dresser, then pulled out a little box full of golden jewelry—a cross, brooch and earrings. She put a finger to her lips, then pointed again at the picture. I thought maybe the Russians, like the Germans, were supposed to relinquish all their gold to the government. Her trust of me, a perfect stranger, made quite an impression on me. The peasants I encountered were often very childlike, hospitable, generous, and trusting. The older people always insisted that I stay with them for more than one night. In one home, I heard a visitor mention Stalin, and the old grandmother said, "Stalin?" and spat on the floor. It amazed me that they dared speak against the government in that manner.

At one home, I watched a wedding from my hiding place, since the people were afraid to reveal me to all their guests. The sound of music and laughter, the sight of people dancing, was so foreign to me, that it was like I had never experienced such gaiety myself. Another time, I witnessed the baptism of a baby, complete with Russian Orthodox priest. I thought it must be a very secretive ceremony, but neighbors filtered in from the surrounding countryside, each bringing a gift for the child. They literally stuffed that baby with food, as part of some tradition, I suppose, and I was glad I wasn't around the next day to see how it must have suffered.

Every time I encountered a religious ceremony or observation in the Russian countryside, I was surprised anew, and inspired, also. I had thought religion was dead in that country, the Communists had argued so strongly with me, but my little cross always meant a welcome for me, and nearly every house I entered had what they called a holy corner that held an icon with a devotion light in front of it. Whenever a slice of bread or meat was cut off for me, the woman of the house made the sign of the cross over the food first. I think that deep in their hearts, each of them has a strong religious feeling, but they are not allowed to express it publicly. I believe that the government will never be able to squelch religion in Russia, because the workers have been a religious people through centuries of war and turmoil, and that devotion cannot be killed in six or seven decades of oppression.

I had only two really bad experiences during all those months of making my way across Russia. The first came not long after I began my trek, when I had to pass through the Ural Mountains. I had stayed with a family for two days, and they told me when I departed that if I went to a certain place, I would be able to hop a freight train as it slowed in its progress up a hill, and that way, make it over the Urals in about two-and-a-half days, rather than spending a week or more walking through them. They even helped me get on the train, but once I was settled in and traveling along at a fast rate, I found that I was not the only hitchhiker aboard. There were two or three men on the same train, hoboes like me, and they had been drinking. Only one of them cared to bother me, but I had to defend myself against him with my little knife and my big temper. Evidently he decided I was too big to argue with, for he went away at last, but after I had fallen asleep from exhaustion, someone stole the bundle of food the farmers had given me. I couldn't stay awake for the whole trip, and as soon as I slept soundly, it was snatched away.

Then, just as I was nearly at the end of my journey, the autumn winds chilled me and I succumbed to a bad cold. I was weak and exhausted. The only strength I retained came from a mental prodding that I was almost home, almost home. Ten days after I collapsed at someone's doorstep, I trudged on down the lane; my rag-bound feet ensconced in an old pair of slippers, still not fully recovered, but determined to go on.

I had reached the frontier between Russia and Finland. The woman who had cared for me during my sickness had pointed in the direction I was headed and warned, "Bang! Bang!" shaking her head and pulling at my arm. The woods near the border were full of mines. The slightest weight would detonate them. I hesitated. What was I to do? Should I listen to these good people and stay with them? I was no longer in prison; I could live here and earn my keep.

No, I have not come this far only to give up. I must, with the help of Christ, make my way through the minefield and on into Finland. It was my only chance of freedom. The last kilometer took me two days. I hardly dared put my foot down. Somehow, I came safely through the mines. I know it was not a feat I could have accomplished on my own. A high barbed wire barrier stood between Finland and me. I dug my way under it with my bare hands, knowing that here, too, there could be mines. I lay on my belly, my face snug against the fresh dirt, inching my way under the bottom strand of wire. My feet cleared and I struggled to my feet, looking about me in a daze. I am in Finland. I stand on Finnish soil. God give me the strength to find help.

I left the clearing and trod through more forest. The first town I came to was Kötka, a harbor with a consulate for each of the countries using her docks. I questioned a number of people I encountered on the street, asking them for the Dutch consulate, but they at first looked at me strangely, then backed away, hurrying off down the street. I had no idea how bad I looked to them. It was late September and I had been traveling afoot since April. I stand five feet, ten inches, yet I weighed, by then, less than a hundred pounds.

Finally, someone showed me the way to an office above a ship supply company. The Dutch Consul himself was Finnish, but he understood German and English, and he was alternately horrified by my story and baffled by what he was going to do with me. He sent me into the waiting room while he called Helsinki, the capital, to find out what to do. But when I tried to do as he bade me, I couldn't get out of the chair. I had reached my goal, left Russia behind, now my strength was gone.

He called an ambulance and I was whisked away to a hospital. The nurses bathed me, holding me upright in the tub, since I could not do so myself, then packed me off to the softest bed in the world. During the next few days, I got more sleep, more injections and more food than I could keep track of. The first thing I ate was some kind of fruit soup—it tasted like raspberries or strawberries with cornstarch and tapioca, accompanied by some kind of light, porous crackers. I graduated to sandwiches in a few days, and I ate constantly.

Escape from Siberia

One of my doctors, a white-haired man with glasses, came in one day and asked how many sandwiches I had eaten since breakfast. "Only twelve," I told him, "and I would like another, if you please."

As soon as I was able to think coherently, I had asked for paper and pen, writing a shaky note to my mother to let her know I was alive, getting well and free. A few days later, the head nurse walked into the ward, waving a single letter above her head. Can it be from Mother, I prayed, and then began to cry with relief as I saw the familiar handwriting. She was 69 then, and I had feared that she would not have survived all those years of war and reconstruction, especially with a heart condition. My last letter to her had been written in the fall of 1944.

Frans is bright and mischievous, and he does very well in school, she wrote. He is always playing tricks on me or your brother, something like his mother used to do. One of my brothers had never married, it turned out, and had remained at home with Mother, acting as a surrogate father for my orphaned child. I read the letter over every day until I had memorized each word, marveling in the strong sureness of Mother's penmanship. I had expected her to be frail and shaky. A photograph of a beautiful little boy with big dark eyes, wavy hair and a straight-backed posture, fell out of an envelope I received the next week. He carried a whistle in his hand, as if he were just getting ready to blow a tune. In another picture, he was sitting in a park, which I recognized from my own childhood. His hair mussed, a pixy grin on his face, a third picture had caught him peering around a corner, as if expecting pursuit and capture following some boyish prank. I bragged on my son and displayed his pictures to everyone in the hospital and the visitors in the garden, and began to pester the doctors about letting me go home. I had been four weeks in the hospital already, building up my strength, and I was anxious to leave.

When I first began to walk around my room, and felt able to go further, I asked a nurse to take me to Mass. It was six o'clock in the morning, and a gorgeous sunrise lit the outside of the church in magenta and gold. She helped me to the first pew, and I stared gratefully at the Eternal Light flickering before me. It is the same. I remembered it right. The priest came through the door of the sacristy and began the prayers in Latin, and I was reminded of my brother, who had become a priest, just as he had predicted when he was 10 years old. There had been nothing else in his mind, but serving the Lord in that way, and he had allowed my sister and me to act as his altar boys when he practiced his youthful sermons. I knew the prayers by heart, and as the Finnish voice spoke the opening words of supplication, "Introibo ad altare Dei" I joined in at the top of my voice, "Ad Deum qui laetificat juventutum meum," tears streaming down my face. Thank God, I am indeed free at last.

I would like to stand on a mountain
And shout out into the wind
So that everyone can hear it,
"I have a child! A child!"

I would like to whisper it in the night
In words tender and mild
So that only I can hear it,
"I have a child. A child."

However much they hurt me,
How much they are against me,
The greatest treasure I keep
Because that is my child.

Johanna

CHAPTER ELEVEN

My son, My son...

I was going home. My letter to Mother, pinpointing the date and time of my arrival in Amsterdam, had been sent. The technicality of being a "non-existent" ward of the state, a foreigner with no passport or identification, a woman without a country, had been cleared up between Finland and Holland. My host government had paid for a new dress, coat, scarf, beret, underclothing, stockings and shoes.

A train took me from Kötka to Helsinki, where a man from the embassy met me and drove me to the airport for a plane ride to Stockholm. The detour through Sweden simplified my entry into Holland, as the Swedes had sheltered many refugees during the war, as a neutral country, and it was commonplace to leave Sweden without the proper papers. At Stockholm's Bromma airport, I was met by another embassy man and taken to the Grand Hotel. Here I was with my single change of clothes and a cardboard suitcase, and I was afraid they might not let me in, but evidently my companion explained the situation, for I was treated with great deference.

I got very little sleep in my luxurious suite, though, because my mind was filled with the homecoming scheduled for the next day. I breakfasted and the attaché arrived to take me back to the airport, my stomach flip-flopping from nerves already, and not improving with the flight to Amsterdam. I had never been in a plane before, yet I paid little attention to the details of the flight, my mind was so occupied with what I would say, how I would act, when I at last would see my son. There was nobody to meet me at the terminal gate. I told myself, don't be silly. They are waiting inside, out of the weather. But they weren't inside either. I was baffled. I mechanically went through exchanging my small amount of Finnish money for Dutch, submitting my letter of explanation from the consulate as to why I didn't have a passport or other papers. I looked around at each sound, each voice in the busy terminal, expecting each time to see Mother or some member of my family. But there was no one.

You know Mother was always embarrassed by public displays of emotion, I reasoned with myself as I left the airport. She probably wanted this to be a private affair, at home, this reunion. But, still, I thought, at least my brother could have come, or one of my sisters.

I took a bus into town, then caught a cab to the railroad station. I bought a ticket to my hometown, and spent the forty-five minute train ride walking through the cars searching for a familiar face, but I knew none of the travelers. I took a taxi out to my mother's house, marveling that the street looked so much the same, and there was the little park where she had taken the picture of Frans.

The door of the old house opened as I was paying the cabfare. Mother's face was red with crying, the tears still rolled down her cheeks. I had never seen her cry. Surely these were not tears of joy for me. This was agonized grief.

"Mama. Mama. Where is Frans?" My skin registered the alarm before the thought fully shaped in my mind, and I shivered involuntarily.

She looked quickly behind her, then put out her hands. "Come in. Sit down."

"Tell me, Mother, where is he?" I was screaming. I grabbed my mother's arms and shook her.

"No. You can go upstairs later. Please..."

I ran past her, through the room and up the steep stairs. I knew where my mother's room was, where my brothers had slept, probably she had made the little guest room into a nursery, then private room for my Frans.

My son lay on top of his bed, his skin pale against the pure white bedcover, dressed in clean pajamas, his hair wet and freshly combed, his hands folded across his tiny chest, his brown eyes closed.

My mother touched me, tried to speak to me.

"No, no, no, it's not true. No, my God, no. Please, I, please, not my baby." I ran to the bed. I tried to open his eyes with my fingers and thumbs. I buried my face in his sweet, damp hair, crushing his precious body against my breast, willing my blood to flow into his still heart, my strength into his chill form.

"Child, this was God's will," my mother tried to console me.

"How can it be?" I asked bitterly, my heart aching, unable to cry. "Haven't I suffered enough in this hell on earth, that he should take my baby away? My child, who gave me the strength to endure all the tortures, all the starvation, all the humiliating, heartbreaking years? What justice is there in this innocent death? Who was it that this sacrifice was made for? What on earth could I have done to cause the death of my only son?"

They tried, Mother and my brother, to take me out of the room, to take my son from my arms, but I fought them. I was beyond reason. I felt nothing but unending, agonizing grief, and the lifeless weight that filled my arms. At some point, the doctor came and helped them wrestle me away from my son's body, to give me a shot for sleeping. I spent the next few days in an exhausted, drugged state. They didn't even let me wake up enough even to attend the funeral. I know I couldn't have gotten through it.

When I had returned to a rational state of mind, Mother told me what had happened. Frans had dressed early in anticipation of meeting me at the airport, this mother he had never seen, but whom he knew so well from the stories he had been told time after time by his uncle and grandmother. Since Mother wasn't ready yet, he asked permission to go into the park with his cousin, who was two years older, to play. The cousin found a bird's nest, which was empty, but my son, a nature lover, knew that the birds would return to it, and told the older boy to leave it where it was. His cousin wanted to tease him, and threatened to throw the nest into the canal that flows through the park. During the course of the tussle over the nest, Frans had stumbled and fallen into the water. He was a good swimmer, but it seems he struck his head on submerged tree roots and was knocked unconscious. A couple across the canal saw him fall, saw his cousin run away in fright and confusion, but they were elderly, and they had to run downstream to a bridge in order to cross the fast-moving water. His body had been recovered only an hour before I came home.

Again, Christ carried me through the blackness of my sorrow. He consoled me, lifted me up from my depression, and convinced me once more that I had something special to live for, that my son was with God and safe from all suffering, that I must continue my quest for knowledge, my growth through Christ. It took me such a long time to accept His message, to be able to say, "Thy will be done". I know my mother prayed daily for me, and I, at last, was able to turn toward Him, instead of away, and add my own prayer for guidance.

"Thy will be done, on earth, as it is in heaven."

> June 30, 1967
>
> I am accepted as a citizen of this great nation. May God help me to contribute to it's goals: liberty and justice for all.
> I'm as proud and as grateful as can be.
>
> Johanna.

Welcome

to you as a

New Citizen

on the occasion of your

Naturalization

M–76
Revised 2–1–67

UNITED STATES DEPARTMENT OF JUSTICE
IMMIGRATION AND NATURALIZATION SERVICE

†

Onze Moeder, Grootmoeder en Overgrootmoeder
MARIA ANNA SOMMERMEIJER
weduwe van
Johan Bernard Köster
Lid van de Derde Orde van Sint Dominicus
is heden gestorven op de leeftijd van 78 jaar.
Zij gaf ons zeer veel liefde, waarvoor wij haar, kinderen, klein- en achterkleinkinderen, oprecht danken en prijzen. Wij zijn bedroefd omdat zij niet meer bij ons is en toch verblijd, omdat zij haar ziel aan onze Hemelse Vader mocht teruggeven na door Hem te zijn gesterkt met zijn laatste genadegaven.

Meerssen:	H. A. A. KÖSTER
	A. KÖSTER-OUD
	kinderen en kleinkinderen
Geleen:	C. E. A. BÜNNEMEIJER-KÖSTER
	L. O. M. BÜNNEMEIJER
	en kinderen
Alkmaar:	TH. M. DE WOLF-KÖSTER
	J. A. J. DE WOLF en kinderen
Bergen N.H.:	A. B. A. KÖSTER
	S. M. C. KÖSTER-HEEGER
	en kinderen
Bergen N.H.:	J. B. KÖSTER
Bêthencourt sur Mer	
Frankrijk:	H. H. KÖSTER pr.
Naarden:	E. A. LUBBERS-KÖSTER
	H. LUBBERS en kinderen
Götheborg	
Zweden:	J. A. KÖSTER

Alkmaar, 24 maart 1960
Emmastraat 10
Huize „St Augustinus"

De gezongen H. Mis van Requiem zal opgedragen worden, maandag 28 maart a.s. te 9.30 uur in de kapel van Huize „St Augustinus", waarna de begrafenis te ± 11 uur in het familiegraf op het R.K. kerkhof „St Barbara" alhier.
Gelegenheid tot condoleren na de H. Uitvaartdienst in Huize „St Augustinus", Emmastraat 10. Rozenkransgebed: 's avonds 7.30 uur in de kapel van Huize „St Augustinus".

Geen bloemen, gaarne H.H. Missen.

EPILOGUE

I moved to Sweden as soon as I was able to function on my own again. I had been impressed by the friendliness of the people when I had been there before, and decided to establish a business of guiding tours for business groups traveling through Denmark, Germany, Holland, Belgium, France, Switzerland and Italy. Every year, I made the trip from my new home to Mother's, as I had promised her. She understood that I could not bear to remain in the house where my son had died, and I had nothing but bitter memories of Germany.

In 1960, my niece wrote that Mother's health was failing and I took a train to Holland. Riding in the same compartment was an American couple who overheard me speaking Swedish to one passenger, German to another, and then English to them. I talked for a long time with them, and they encouraged me to move to the United States, where my knowledge of European languages could qualify me for a high-paying job. I explained that I had an obligation to my mother, which they understood, but before we parted, the man said, "If you ever change your mind, here is my business card. Maybe I could do something to help you."

"If I did decide to come, I would need a sponsor, " I ventured, my mind just beginning to accept all the possibilities America could have for me. He assured me that he would consider it an honor and a privilege to sponsor me, and his wife added, "You can live with us in Pasadena, until you find something to do."

My mother died only a month later, in March 1960. In April, I wrote the American couple, asking them if they remembered their offer and were still willing to help me. Their response was enthusiastic and I applied for my U.S. visa in June, but it took me until February 1962 to get it. A requirement to supply papers from every town I had lived in for more than six months since I was 16 years old complicated matters, and I had to supply a lot of sworn statements as to why I could not account for all the years of my life, in reference to Dutch residency. My suitcases had been packed for weeks before I was finally able to leave. I had sold my business, given up my apartment. I was anxious to go ahead with my plans for a new life. Without Mother to hold me in Europe, I could think of nothing better than putting an entire ocean between the nightmares of Germany, the KGB of Russia and me and me.

I came to my new country by way of Icelandic Airlines, Loftleidir, over Oslo, Heklavik, Newfoundland, on to New York. An accident at International caused us to re-route to La Guardia, and a bus took us, back to International to go through customs. As I stepped down from the bus, a man in uniform spoke, and I turned with a smile. "You're a Dutchman, aren't you? I can tell by your voice." It seemed an omen that the first person I met on American soil was from my mother country.

I stayed in New York for just over a week, contacting various transplanted Dutch with messages from their relatives in Holland. A lady I met as I was out for a walk took me to St. Dominic's, to see the Empire State Building and Cardinal Spellman, and explained to me that all the boxes hanging on the sides of the American buildings were air conditioners. A priest staying at the same hotel knew my brother, and when I reached Missouri, a slight detour on my way west, one of the nuns I met there had bought her coats at my father's store before she had become a nun and moved to America. It was unbelievable, the people I met who knew someone I had known, or was related to. Each stop brought me more new friends, and they always knew somebody in the next town "on my way" who would love to have me stay over, or who would feel neglected if I didn't stop by with a greeting or message from so-and-so.

In that manner, I made my way across the states to my friends in Pasadena, to whom I remain so grateful. If I had become destitute, been unable to work, they would have taken care of me forever, I knew, but luckily, I was able to make it on my own. I never had to ask for a handout.

I had to wait five years to apply for naturalization. My application was filed in February 1967; in April, I took the test; I was sworn in on a beautiful June day. Everyone in the company where I worked joined me in celebration of my achievement. They gave me an Uncle Sam's hat and an American flag, and I marched through the plant singing, inviting everyone to help me eat the cake that proclaimed "Congratulations and Welcome, New Citizen".

Poor health forced me to retire in 1977, and I came to Oregon at the invitation of a bishop. It is paradise to me, this land of fresh air, green timber and miles of open space. I can be close to the outdoors, the animals, and I have found everything here that I need to make me happy: faith, serenity, friends and peace of mind.

The older I get, the happier I am.

Johanna with Hanzie, her devoted Cocker Spaniel—a great pair.
One just as mischievous as the other.

POSTSCRIPT

I was the lucky Bishop who had invited Johanna to come to Oregon in 1977. She worked at various private homes taking care of elderly women. She took care of all their needs. Many of them were bedridden and helpless and Johanna cared for them like a mother would care for her child. She spoke to them all about the love of God. She did not hesitate to share her Catholic faith with all who cared to listen. "I am a strong Catholic," she would say.

She also communicated an infectious warmth of affection. One day, towards the end of her life, I visited her at Saint Elizabeth Hospital in Baker. She smacked her lips when I approached her bed and so I kissed her. A few moments later when a nurse came in she said in a loud mischievous voice, "I kissed the Bishop and I scared the hell out of him."

About a week later on March 27th, 1999, I closed her eyes peacefully in death and a moment later she was pounding on Saint Peter's gate demanding entry. I lost a great friend and I hope you have found a new one.

✝ Bishop Thomas J. Connolly